Praise for *The Best Ame*

"Each year, a vivid snapshot of what a distinguished poet finds exciting, fresh, and memorable: and over the years, as good a comprehensive overview of contemporary poetry as there can be."

—Robert Pinsky

"The *Best American Poetry* series has become one of the mainstays of the poetry publication world. For each volume, a guest editor is enlisted to cull the collective output of large and small literary journals published that year to select seventy-five of the year's 'best' poems. The guest editor is also asked to write an introduction to the collection, and the anthologies would be indispensable for these essays alone; combined with [David] Lehman's 'state-of-poetry' forewords and the guest editors' introductions, these anthologies seem to capture the zeitgeist of the current attitudes in American poetry."

—Academy of American Poets

"A high volume of poetic greatness . . . in all of these volumes . . . there is brilliance, there is innovation, there are surprises."

—*Publishers Weekly* (starred review)

"A year's worth of the very best!"

—*People*

"A preponderance of intelligent, straightforward poems."

—*Booklist*

"Certainly it attests to poetry's continuing vitality."

—*Publishers Weekly* (starred review)

"A 'best' anthology that really lives up to its title."

—*Chicago Tribune*

"An essential purchase."

—*The Washington Post*

"For the small community of American poets, *The Best American Poetry* is the *Michelin Guide*, the *Reader's Digest*, and the Prix Goncourt."

—*L'Observateur*

THE
BEST
AMERICAN
POETRY
2022

◇ ◇ ◇

Matthew Zapruder, Editor

David Lehman, Series Editor

SCRIBNER POETRY

NEW YORK LONDON TORONTO SYDNEY NEW DELHI

Scribner Poetry
An Imprint of Simon & Schuster, Inc.
1230 Avenue of the Americas
New York, NY 10020

First Scribner edition September 2022

SCRIBNER POETRY and design are registered trademarks of The Gale Group, Inc.,
used under license by Simon & Schuster, Inc., the publisher of this work.

For information about special discounts for bulk purchases,
please contact Simon & Schuster Special Sales at 1-866-506-1949
or business@simonandschuster.com.

The Simon & Schuster Speakers Bureau can bring authors to
your live event. For more information or to book an event,
contact the Simon & Schuster Speakers Bureau at 1-866-248-3049
or visit our website at www.simonspeakers.com.

Manufactured in the United States of America

1 3 5 7 9 10 8 6 4 2

Library of Congress Control Number: 88644281

ISBN 978-1-9821-8669-2
ISBN 978-1-9821-8668-5 (pbk)
ISBN 978-1-9821-8670-8 (ebook)

CONTENTS

DAVID LEHMAN was born in New York City. Educated at Stuyvesant High School and Columbia University, he spent two years at Clare College, Cambridge, as a Kellett Fellow, and worked as Lionel Trilling's research assistant upon his return from England. *The Mysterious Romance of Murder: Crime, Detection, and the Spirit of Noir* is forthcoming from Cornell University Press. Other recent books include *The Morning Line* (University of Pittsburgh Press, 2021), a book of poems, and *One Hundred Autobiographies: A Memoir* (Cornell, 2019). He is the editor of *The Oxford Book of American Poetry* (2006) and has written nonfiction books on critical theory in higher education, the New York School of poets, American jazz standards, and Frank Sinatra. In 2010 he received the Deems Taylor Award from the American Society of Composers, Authors, and Publishers (ASCAP). Lehman launched *The Best American Poetry* series in 1988. A gathering of the forewords he had written for the series appeared in 2015 under the title *The State of the Art: A Chronicle of American Poetry, 1988–2014*. A contributing editor of *The American Scholar*, Lehman lives in New York City and in Ithaca, New York.

FOREWORD

by David Lehman

◇ ◇ ◇

Years ago the rumor circulated that secretly it was I who picked the poems for the annual *Best American Poetry*. Perhaps I should have felt flattered. Did I really wield so much power and influence? Did anyone seriously believe that I could dictate to Charles Simic, Adrienne Rich, John Hollander, Rita Dove, Robert Creeley, et al? On the face of it, the notion was absurd. *The guest editor chooses the poems.* His or her autonomy is guaranteed as a ground condition, and we go to pains to emphasize this fact.

I esteem the poems in this year's *Best American* not just for their particular virtues but precisely because they are the picks of Matthew Zapruder, whose knowledge of poetry today makes him an ideal witness. Some of my own favorite poems of the year are in these pages, but some that didn't make the cut deserve acknowledgment, and I would like to draw attention to them here.

Poetry is sometimes newsworthy, as when a "new" poem by a great writer comes to light. In March 2021, London's *Times Literary Supplement* published a 1942 poem by Vladimir Nabokov that previously only a few scholars had read. A lover of Superman, the comic-book hero that a pair of Cleveland lads, Joe Shuster and Jerry Siegel, concocted, Nabokov wrote "The Man of To-morrow's Lament" at the suggestion of his friend Edmund Wilson. Superman, the speaker of the poem, contemplates the dire predicament that threatens his romantic life:

> I'm young and bursting with prodigious sap,
> and I'm in love like any healthy chap—
> and I must throttle my dynamic heart
> for marriage would be murder on my part,

an earthquake, wrecking on the night of nights
a woman's life, some palmtrees, all the lights,
the big hotel, a smaller one next door
and half a dozen army trucks—or more.

Even worse would ensue if somehow his romantic partner survived and a "monstrous babe" was born to them. That is why, he tells us, he gets gloomy whenever he "tucks away" the "red-cloaked, blue-hosed" uniform of Superman and dons the coat and trousers of Clark Kent. There's a statue of him in Central Park. But "I stare ahead / and long to be a normal guy instead."

An example of the mock heroic as practiced by such as Alexander Pope in *The Rape of the Lock*, Nabokov's bawdy poem—composed by a nonnative speaker of English who had only recently arrived in America—is steeped in the conventions of poetry. Scrupulously rhymed, the poem alludes to *King Lear*—Clark Kent is "a banished trunk (like my namesake in 'Lear')"—and makes a knowing aside about Berchtesgaden, the Bavarian Alps retreat favored by Hitler. But the most striking thing about "The Man of To-morrow's Lament" is that Nabokov puts his erudition and sophisticated technique to the service of a bubble-gum fantasy that captured the imagination of young people at the dawn of an era that idealized youth culture. In a sense the poem is a prelude to the romance of adolescence in Nabokov's most famous novel, *Lolita*. Considered in the light of Pop Art in general and Roy Lichtenstein's paintings in particular, "The Man of To-morrow's Lament" is a prophesy of what took the art world by storm in the 1960s.

In 1942 Nabokov submitted the poem to *The New Yorker*. Charles Pearce, the magazine's poetry editor, rejected it. In addition to the risqué element, he wrote, "Most of us appear to feel that many of our readers wouldn't quite get it."

Two poems I admired deal with technology and the changes it has both undergone and forced upon us during the COVID-19 pandemic. "Zoom Rooms," Mary Jo Salter's sequence of sonnets in the spring 2021 issue of *The American Scholar*, looks at "real life at a social distance." With rhymes and half-rhymes Salter makes the effort to come to terms with, and maybe even vitalize, the new jargon. She contends with "zoom" itself, "unmute" ("a word I might dispute / even exists, whether verb or adjective"), "gallery view," and generational tags, such as "Boomer," "Millennial," and "Generation C / for coronavirus." The level of wit in "Zoom Rooms" reminds me that John Donne audaciously used a mathematical instrument as a messenger of love. Consider:

> Depending on the scale of your device,
> the size of a single Zoomed-in human soul
> is that of a sonnet: modest and concise.

The poem is, among other things, a self-portrait in a Zoom room:

> Bookcase-prop and real or fake bouquet
> behind you, well-dressed only to the waist
> as if in a casket, top half on display,
> here's another weirdness to be faced:
> you're in the Gallery. You're shown as one
> of your own satellites—as if the sun
> were both a planet and the Copernican
> magnet for all planets.

The word "cloud" has acquired a meaning unanticipated by Wordsworth in "I Wandered Lonely as a Cloud" or the Rolling Stones in "Get Off of My Cloud." Rachel Hadas, who teaches at Rutgers, found herself conducting her course in "Reading Poetry" via Zoom. In "In the Cloud," which enlivened the May 24, 2021, issue of *The New Yorker*, Hadas modifies her doubts with joyous rhymes while thinking out loud about the faces on the computer screen:

> What does this mean to you? I said.
> What does *beautiful* really mean?
> I asked them as I tried to lean
> into the noncommittal screen,
> scanning until my eyes were sore

for the soul in each black square.
Were there really people there?
Did each name hide a secret face
sheltering somewhere in place,
some unimaginable space?

Here's how the poem sums up the current state of communal life in virtual space: "Alone together, here we are, / stranded in our shared nowhere."

To enlarge the sphere of poetry, to keep up with the acceleration of change, to incorporate the age's new materials and lexicon is a daunting task, and I applaud Salter and Hadas for tackling it with formidable intelligence. To confront the new with one of poetry's most traditional devices, rhyme, is a daring move.

Old age, its torments and compensations, may not be quite as resistant to verse as high-tech gadgetry, but it is generally neglected or treated in the context of obituary or elegy. Wordsworth, who was unusual in the sympathy he displayed for old men encountered by chance on his walks, wrote: "We Poets in our youth begin in gladness; / But thereof come in the end despondency and madness." Does this sad progress remain the case? Do we pay enough attention to poets who are writing their best work in their seventies?

If part of the poet's job is to take a difficult condition and render it exactly but with a certain balancing lightheartedness, Terence Winch does so addressing what he has called "old life" in "That Ship Has Sailed," which was published online in *Across the Margin*. The poem consists of two stanzas, the first of which is ebullient in evoking "our" youth in accents recalling Keats's definition of negative capability. What did "we" read?

Keats and Yeats and all the greats
day and night. We got into fights
in pubs. We drank sixteen cups
of coffee every day. We called in sick
and spent the day in mysteries, doubts,
uncertainties.

The much-shorter second section begins with memory loss but ends not with the senior moments you might expect but with glorious ritual and rich metaphor:

> . . . We light a candle
> to commemorate crossing
> the great divide between
> the green island of the young
> and the songs in our bones
> that have come unsung.

A friend introduced me to Teri Ellen Cross Davis's poem "*Bad Girls Album Cover*," which celebrates the sensuality of Donna Summer as depicted "under a / streetlamp's maraschino cherry glow," with wet black ringlets framing "her light brown-sugared face," and "pouting lips"

> slick in shiny scarlet gloss, high heel perched on the lamp's base
> plunging the slit of her dress back to reveal a black lace stocking
>
> a garter as garnish   so naughty, so beautiful.

Poets are celebrating the erotic. They are also exercising the right to court a comic muse. Angela Ball's "Mississippi State's Football Coach Ponders the Fake People in the Stands" makes merry with the coach's public statement about playing before a crowd of cardboard cutouts:

> It's science fiction meets haunted stadium:
> you're watching the big game, and you can't move,
> let alone cheer or boo. If it's cool,
> and people enjoy it, great, but it's a little
> surreal, the fake people in the stands.
>
> Do the person impersonators have a lottery
> to see who gets the best seats? Some have way better ones,
> those fake people in the stands.

Speaking of sports, I had no idea that the late Dan Quisenberry, the relief ace of the Kansas City Royals in the 1980s, wrote poems until Paul Worley, the poetry editor of *North Dakota Quarterly*, published six of them. Three deal directly with baseball and reveal a sensibility that a sportswriter would envy. "Time to Quit" is set in San Francisco. The pitcher is trying to warm up, but

> It's a damp wind-off-the-water cold
> and I'm trying to throw sinkers
> into this gale force
> the ball
> a sparrow in a hurricane
> barely makes it.

"The first time I read these I felt like I was sitting down with an old friend I admittedly only knew via the medium of baseball cards, televised games, and my own dollar store imitations of [Quisenberry's distinctive pitching] delivery," Worley says. He is right to characterize the poems as "deep, moving, complicated," the confidences of a man who "used to be famous," as Quisenberry puts it in "Baseball Cards":

> I used to be good
> they say
> we thought you were bigger
> I say
> I was

If I were the guest editor of this volume, I would also pick something by Matthew Zapruder.

★

Twenty-one years ago, at a literary festival organized by James Tate and Dara Wier at the University of Massachusetts, I met Matthew and was immediately taken by his enthusiasm and by the quality of his poems. I have observed him as an instructor at The New School, as the co-director of the Monday-night poetry readings series at KGB Bar, and as an editor at large of Wave Books. I am not alone in admiring his work. David Wagoner, Denise Duhamel, Natasha Trethewey, and Paisley Rekdal chose poems by Zapruder for the 2009, 2013, 2017, and 2020 editions of this series. Terrance Hayes, in his note about "The Rose Has Teeth," which Mark Doty selected for *BAP 2012*, wrote that his own poem "found its bones after I read Matthew Zapruder's marvelous poem, 'Never to Return,' in the 2009 edition of *The Best American Poetry*."

When I learned that Amy Gerstler, who made the choices for *BAP 2010*, felt as I did about Zapruder's work, I asked her to write about a poem she admired. She responded with dispatch. "The poem 'My Life,' from Matthew Zapruder's 2019 book *Father's Day* is emblematic of what's heart-expanding about his work. Composed predominately of two- and three-word lines with minimal punctuation, the poem is a halting outpouring (if that's not too oxymoronic a phrase), a quiet, unresolved struggle with emotional recalculation and acceptance. 'My Life' is a double origin story, a poem in which the speaker recounts both his son's conception and birth and his own sea change/ rebirth as he becomes not just a father but parent of a neurodivergent child. 'My Life' begins with the protagonist and his wife trying to conceive: 'four years ago / on Martin Luther King Day / in the afternoon / the little strip / said it was time.' The poem progresses through 'the year / of diagnosis when / our life kept / being a place for worsening fears,' to 'then came the proud / sleepless happy / sorrow months.' As evidenced in these lines, an obsession with time is one of the poem's engines.

"Despite its title it's hard to label 'My Life' confessional because the poem exercises so much discretion, and never loses sight of its own subjectivity. Rather than make that subjectivity a central tenet, as confessional poems from the past often do, 'My Life' keeps doubling back and interrogating itself. The poem's tone of confiding worry is leavened with humor, self-awareness, and a hard-won tenderness that rises through the poem, eventually overtaking, or at least, by the end, running neck and neck with its sadness and fears. Zapruder has a unique ability to ponder contemporary life's specific predicaments (ethical, personal, and political) with radical humility and chastened hope."

That I rely on the guest editors I have worked with must be evident from my many references to them in this foreword. Sadly we lost two in 2021. Robert Bly, who made the selections for *BAP 1999*, died in November. He was ninety-four. It was he who gave me the idea of writing a poem each day, which is what he was doing in January 1996, the coldest January in years at Bennington College. He wrote first thing in the morning, while curtains remained drawn. He would sit up in bed, in close contact with what he called his reptilian brain, and write at a time when travel across the Maginot Line of consciousness went both ways on uncongested highways and took unpredictable turns—not a metaphor Bly would have liked, by the way, not only because he didn't go to history for his rhetoric but also because, dreadful as it was, the world did not face what France faced in May 1940. Robert liked images—a turtle, a spear, an onion, a castle—and wishes, like the desire to travel far or to be in Paris on a Thursday on your last day alive. A big man, the author of "The Teeth Mother Naked at Last" among other arresting titles, he vigorously promoted the prose poem as a form or genre. He advanced his ideas about masculinity in *Iron John: A Book About Men*, a fixture on best-seller lists for more than a year. Robert was said to be cantankerous but I found him generous, loyal, an excellent teacher and raconteur, and it was a joy to walk with him—and to work with him on *The Best American Poetry 1999*.

On December 18, David Wagoner, the guest editor of *The Best American Poetry 2009*, died in his sleep at the age of ninety-six. When he read for the series he was, at eighty-two, the oldest of our guest editors, and yet one of the most assiduous in monitoring the landscape and representing the entire range of American poetry. In his introduction to the anthology, David wrote: "Why do people write poems? There are probably a hundred answers to that question, maybe more, but some writers feel they have important messages to give mankind, and of course they usually turn out to be strangely inaudible to that vast audience. Some people just like to play around with words as they might with jigsaw puzzles or pinball machines. Some indulge themselves with poetry secretly, in words as private as diary entries. For some it's a form of public speaking, and they look for audiences in social clubs, or open mics, or even on street corners, making themselves heard to strangers. Some hear their own voices and the voices of other people speaking to them in half sleep and feel obliged to write down what they say in order to understand their own existence more fully. For a number of them what starts out to be a kind of game turns out to be the most complex and rewarding of all game-like activities, something more nearly religious, as demanding and baffling and compelling as ethics, metaphysics, the search for a god, or even love."

MATTHEW ZAPRUDER was born in Washington, D.C., in 1967. An Amherst College graduate, he studied Slavic languages at UC Berkeley and received an MFA in poetry from the University of Massachusetts. *American Linden*, his first book, was published by Tupelo Press in 2002. He has written four collections since, including *Come On All You Ghosts* (Copper Canyon Press, 2010), a *New York Times* Notable Book of the Year, and most recently *Father's Day* (Copper Canyon, 2019). *Why Poetry*, a book of prose about reading poetry for a general audience, was published by Ecco Press in 2017. In 2000, he cofounded Verse Press, and is now editor at large at Wave Books, where he edits contemporary poetry, prose, and translations. In collaboration with Radu Ioanid, he translated *Secret Weapon: The Late Poems of Eugen Jebeleanu* (Coffee House Press, 2008). His poetry has been adapted and performed at Carnegie Hall. From 2016 to 2017 Zapruder, a former Guggenheim Fellow, held the annually rotating position of editor of the poetry column for *The New York Times Magazine*. He lives in the San Francisco Bay Area, where he teaches in the MFA program in creative writing at Saint Mary's College of California.

INTRODUCTION

by Matthew Zapruder

◇　◇　◇

If you are reading this and don't read much poetry, or feel uncertain in relation to it, you are more than welcome here. Maybe you are browsing in a bookstore, or have been assigned this book for a class, or have received it as a gift. Please know that I chose these poems thinking of you. I, too, feel uncertain, unsure of what poetry is for, especially during eerie, frightening, and confusing times. But finding these seventy-five poems helped me, and I hope they will help you, too.

Maybe you go to art, as I do, because you find that there, unlike in so much of the rest of life, people are asking the big questions. They don't already know the answers and are not necessarily trying to convince us of something, but we can be with them while they are searching. In poems, I often hear a solitary consciousness trying to ask hard questions, to make some sense of things without oversimplifying them, to share the experience of thinking through something in ways that are not beholden to convention.

In poems, language—humanity's greatest invention—is liberated. I think this is what people often mean when they say they want to be surprised by a poem, not only by its content, and not by mere decoration of that content, but by a feeling of possibility itself, manifested in language. As García Lorca wrote, "I do not believe in creation but in discovery, and I don't believe in the seated artist but in the one who is walking down the road."

It's amazing how the old technology of the lyric can still push everything else away and create a dangerous space of possibility. There seem to be an infinite number of ways to do it; at least so far no one has discovered the limit. As I was reading through all the magazines and websites in 2021, I did not have preconceived ideas about what I was looking for. I wanted a feeling of resonance in me that something necessary and true was being said, and by "necessary" I mean necessary to say in just this way. Lift your head from your device, and I will lift my head from mine.

These are dire times. Often the question occurred to me, reading all these poems: *What am I doing?* Certain poems reminded me that there was possibility in language and thought, which gave me some hope. Yet I often felt convinced that none of this literary activity was going to make the slightest difference.

What gave me hope was the sense that everywhere people are still dreaming. We can't help it. The dream is the place where one is free to imagine anything. It is beyond our usual means of control and is uninterested in the limits of what has been considered possible. As Delmore Schwartz wrote, "In dreams begin responsibilities." Audre Lorde wrote that "it is through poetry that we give names to those ideas which are—until the poem—nameless and formless, about to be birthed, but already felt." Maybe all this reading and writing is not merely useful, but essential.

The poetic imagination connects concretely with activism, resistance, and optimism. A hope that starts out as a tentative, inchoate feeling can, in a poem, be dreamed forth, envisioned as a concrete possibility; only then, when we start to imagine how things could change, can we begin to act to make it so.

The Surrealists saw dreams as essential to ending war, and to improving the human condition. Emerging from the horrors of World War I, they believed that if everyone wrote poetry, the dream world would be linked once again to what we call everyday reality; if that happened, we would no longer see each other as machines. It would be the end of cruelty and conflict. As we now know, the horrors of the twentieth century were only beginning. But the Surrealists were not wrong that dreaming is at least a step toward change. A poem is a dream made manifest in the world, for oneself and others. Before we dismiss dreams as a source of knowledge and power and change, we should remember that Dr. Martin Luther King Jr. did not say he had a thought, or a plan, or an idea.

In this year of pandemic, we do not need any reminders to grieve or to feel love or compassion. Yet perhaps you found yourself growing numb, as I did. The imagination of these poets took me again and again to places where I could feel again, though not in the usual ways. Often the poems painfully reminded me that everything is alive. A bulldozer lowers its bucket in the rain. When a goldfish dies, we mourn the entire ocean. A bolt of lightning falls in love. Our love, like our grief, is unreasoned.

The poems I love most are responsible to others and the world but also feel free. "If I am not for myself, who will be? And if I am only for myself, what am I? And if not now, when?" said Hillel the Elder. Today we are living in the ultimate paradox of those words. Conflicts between self and other, the role of the individual in relation to community, the responsibility of ourselves to others and to the earth— these are the sites of unending failures and disappointments. Many of our contemporary poems enter into that conflict between the self and the collective—not to resolve it, which would be impossible, but to clarify our position.

Vievee Francis looks at a photograph of poet Galway Kinnell being held by Harriet Richardson after state troopers beat him at the march from Selma to Montgomery. This photograph of a bleeding white man held by a black woman at a march against racial discrimination could, in lesser hands, easily become a dangerous site of sentimentality. It's a beautiful photograph, in its confusion. Francis uses it to explore, in a relatively small space, questions of race, especially as they relate to her own interracial marriage. From her perspective she observes the desire of white men (Kinnell and her husband) to be compassionate, and the limits of that desire. She imagines Richardson's emotions and gives us a chronicle of her own. It's hard for me to imagine an essay many times the length of this poem investigating such matters with as much clarity and insight, and, perhaps most important, respect for the limits of understanding.

The poems in this volume, to which I returned again and again, and that I could not and did not want to move on from or forget, seemed to be searching as in a dream for something not easily said or known. These poems are active, full of a spirit of questioning, searching for a different way of being. Jericho Brown's "Inaugural" feels like a far more accurate assessment of the American condition than any speech or editorial or sermon:

We were told that it is dangerous to touch
And yet we journeyed here, where what we believe
Meets what must be done. You want to see, in spite
Of my mask, my face. We imagine, in time

Of disease, our grandmothers
Whole. We imagine an impossible
America and call one another
A fool for doing so. . . .

Here is the virus, both literal and metaphoric, which makes it "dangerous to touch." Brown's poem acknowledges the impossible desire to see past the mask of the face, for dreams to bring back the dead, and for America somehow to become what it purports to be—to live up to its ideals, which, as Brown writes, we cannot help but imagine and hope for, even though we are fools for doing so.

His description of the American dilemma, of the dual nature of our dreams, which are both self-deluding and full of necessary hope, is ruthlessly accurate. And complex. It requires reading and rereading with a mind that is willing to be plastic in relation to the intuitions and leaps made by the poem. Only a poem, it seems to me, is capable of expressing and creating, in the mind of the reader, the coexisting, colliding, disappointing, irresolvable mess of despair, rage, and foolish hope that defines what it is to be American.

In these poems I was drawn to pattern-making in the material of language and structure of the poems themselves, usually more subtle than overt, like the faint echo of phrasal rhythms or the low hum of sonic similarity. Poets are also interested in patterns of experience and meaning, and in finding those commonalities where they are utterly unexpected.

Poets, like all artists, continually emerge from the privacy of their own anomalies into a collective space, which makes poems inherently hopeful for human connection. Poems remind us that, at our core, we share something deep. This is the gorgeous paradox of poetry. It's as if there are human qualities that link us across time and geographical and other differences. Perhaps this is ultimately a fiction, but poems make use of that hope of commonality while reminding us of the individuality of perception—how far we are away from each other, how singular experience is, how weird and unpredictable and inappropriate we are. The assertion of individuality in the poems in this anthology, coexisting with a belief that it is possible to find common ground, constitutes a kind of implicit hope that we might, despite all that separates us, find a way to pull together to solve the grave problems that threaten us all.

Many of these poems engage with the central conflicts and dilemmas of our time, always in interesting and new ways. It's more than okay though if sometimes these poems are about private matters like mustaches, and rhinestones, and love. They remind us of what we will need to fight for. In "The Life of a Writer," Jalynn Harris writes:

> . . . how deep in love i am
>
> & how silly of me to spend all morning dreaming
> about love & not expect my
>   desire to set me free
>
> the knives of my fingers tap
> out the notion that if i turn the key
>   it will unlock.

This poet is writing about writing about love. I like that she admits that it feels silly, though of course it is not. It might be the most important thing in the world. She wants to understand, to explore, to know. She is trying to get closer to human experience by writing and thinking. Her fingers are knives; there is a key; there is something that will unlock. Yes.

Would you imagine your fingers are knives, especially in the moment of typing a poem about love? I would not. Now I will not forget it. Aristotle wrote that metaphor is the "application of an alien name": it makes a connection that is inherently unexpected or unauthorized, but in retrospect seems to have been waiting there all along. That is the rebellious spirit by which poets are animated.

Despite all the efforts to control it, poetry has from the beginning never bent to authority. Poets are constantly breaking the rules, to reveal what should be considered beautiful and therefore worth preserving. Which means that the most important elements of the best poems might not be immediately understood as poetry. The inclusion of these disparate, unpredictable, misbehaving elements in the same space expands our sense of what is possible. What we thought was strange or took for granted or did not see as beautiful—or even see at all, before the poem—becomes something we cannot live without. The greatest poems demand change. Maybe we need to change to meet them.

Sometimes I think of poems less as artifacts of individual minds, and more as a part of a collective effort. Poets are specialists in the unknown, and because of the compactness of a poem and its flexibility, can respond rapidly to any situation. After a dose of truth serum most poets will admit they write mostly by instinct, or as Frank O'Hara said, "You just go on your nerve." This makes poets suited to dramatic moments in history, which no one can make sense of while they are happening. Shelley wrote that poets don't really even understand what they are saying. He meant this as a compliment. By singing, poets turn themselves into instruments that don't just reflect their times, but also tell the future, becoming "mirrors of the gigantic shadows which futurity casts upon the present."

Is this book a time capsule? A futile cry into a dark future? A harbinger of necessary change? A seed bank? A catalog of soon-to-be-anachronistic neuroses? One of the final exhales of literature's expired, propped-up corpse? More kindling? I don't know. I do know that when life is confusing and difficult, we need to encounter it directly. That's what these seventy-five poems do. They are aware of where they sit in relation to others and the world. So many of them feel as if they were written in a growing sense of their own precarity—often in a social sense, but spiritually, too. Like all lyrics that seem true to me, they speak against power with anger or passion or despair or sometimes with an exhilarating disinterest in what is usually considered important. They seem written *against*, in order to preserve.

When I read a poem I love, despite my anger and despair, something in me starts to bloom. Maybe it was already there. Maybe it is something new. The point is, it was only potential before I read the poem. Now I am more alive and aware. I feel sadder, more vulnerable, and more capable of resisting. This puts me in solidarity with my fellow beings. There are many more things to lose, maybe everything, but what I can lose is named. Everything matters more, which is of course terrifying, but at least it is a true condition. In the direst circumstances, poems are available to everyone, and can help us resist, and survive, and see and forgive each other and ourselves.

THE
BEST
AMERICAN
POETRY
2022

America

◇   ◇   ◇

America the footsteps of your ghosts are white stones weighting my center

America the old girls' campus in the heart of Oakland where I teach
  Grows quiet as glass marbles rolling between my feet

I pick one up, I say *It's pretty*
  And my students laugh, cheering *Welcome to America*

I have no one to look to this summer, I light a candle, burn the
  proposedly holy wood

And God does not come when summoned

Just the scent of bonfire in my hair
Gold light flooding the bay window sure as a divination

America I divine nothing

In the other country, my parents wear their silence like silk robes each
  morning, devoted to the terrible sun

Day after day, I weep on the phone, saying, *Even the classroom is a prison*
  And still my father insists *But it is good to become an American*

And so I cement my semantics
I practice my pronunciations, I learn to say *This country*
After saying *I love*

I rinse my aquiline face, wring my language for fear

I feared what had happened in your forest, the words that pursued the
    soft silk of spiders

The verbs were *naturalize, charge, reside*
The nouns were *clematis, alien, hibiscus*

America I arrived to inhabit the realm of your language
        I came to worry your words

What you offered is a vintage apartment, an audience for poems
        Pills the color of dusk
            To swallow so as not to collapse when I read the poem about
            my uncle

The reading of which I owe him, to everyone who antecedes me

No, I mean who *haunts* me

The haunting of which is a voice

The West is too young to be haunted, an ex-lover assures

Still, every night I listen to your voice scraping against my walls

And in the mornings, trivial offerings on my pillows
        I pick the spiders from my bed, flush their curled transparence
            down the drain

America I don't know what to make of my ordinary cruelty
        Or my newly bourgeois pain

Venom lacing each crack of the historic apartment
        Venom lacing the porcelain plates we hand out at parties

In the hallway I let someone touch me under my mask
        Three fingers in my mouth
        My back pushed against the door, the cold sink

The mind plays where it leads, a dark hour, the weight of a body on
    indigo tiles

America the scale says *not thin enough*

America my lawyer suggests to keep quiet about certain things
        About you and me

So I write in my notebook your name, I write *Country of
Cowboys and Fame*

America I have no cowboy
And I have no fame

All I gather is the scratching of ink against paper, the laugh of a skeptic

There are nights we hear something likened to fireworks lighting up
    the humid campus
And my students cheer, they laugh *Welcome to America*

Later in the empty corridor, the disembodied voice of my uncle

Saying   *The classroom is not a prison*
Saying   *Go, go home now* and so I go

Past vetiver and cedar, past eucalyptus declaring the shoreline

Until I shiver on the soft-stoned coast on which my father once lay
        And I proclaim what he did, I say *This land is my fate*

America who am I becoming here with you
        If I wander the same as without you, barely visible amid your
            indigenous trees

from *Poetry*

Text and Image

◇ ◇ ◇

Text and Image

Tabitha: *y haven't u told me u luv me*
Raymond: *I'm literally writing you love poems*

you're trying to send me a portrait
of a lady on fire but the link won't load

so I don't know what it shows
and you're in the cinema rustling

in the dark and we think we aren't
doing things the old way, our marriage

is new age, no more you complete me crap,
have your own life and I have my life

and it's tricky and easy while we're doing
long distance but how can I show you

my love is unfolding if my words
can't reach you glowing and wild?

Text and Image

Raymond: *in the dream I was in a packed cinema.*
I had a remote for the screen, I flick channels,

turn on captions and no one seemed to mind.
Some forgotten Macaulay Culkin film came on

and laughter erupted, then a film trailer started.
I'm on screen talking to the camera but what I'm saying

isn't subtitled. Behind me, a man in a hood
wearing a strange shiny blue tracksuit, he takes off

his hood and it's Macaulay Culkin! He's looking around
and sees me looking at him and quickly puts his hood back on.

A woman with a wide chin is sitting next to me making hmm noises.
On screen, I'm peering up a faintly lit staircase and all goes grainy.

I see that the tattoos on my arm are just scribbled pen marks
then the wide chin woman, realising it's me on the screen, says

you know, you really missed an opportunity,
you're talking about your mother

but you're not really talking about your mother
and I turn to see my mother's face flickering in and out of light.

Text and Image

Tabitha: *Dreamt I was in my studio,*
conserving this painting, slowly sharpening scalpels.

I'm neat and focused until my fingernails
became a large feeling that the painting couldn't understand me.

Meanwhile my fingernails start scratching the canvas,
I lose it and hold the painting, tearing the whole thing in half.

Then there are twelve more paintings at my feet
(Warhol's, Marclay's, Hockney's) and I'm picking up each

and tearing and tearing until my finger nails fell off, became swords
and all the paintings became my uncle (who was murdered)

but there was no blood on his body, just bright blue
and yellow paint and someone kept saying

master, master, master, master, master.

from *The Rumpus*

Remembering

◇ ◇ ◇

As if every time you did it
You started beeping
To warn others not to get run over
By your memories
As if every time you did it
You started thinking
To warn others not to get run over
By your memories
As if every time you did it
You started weeping
As if every time
You started bleeding
By your memories
Just enough to warn others not to get run over

After an agitated night of epic nightmares populated by strangers by the thousands who know everything about me I've never known or have forgotten; after finding in a marked-up copy of Gaston Bachelard's POETICS OF SPACE a note to myself printed in blue ink, in all caps MARKED WITH THE SIGN OF THE FIRST TIME; another note in script There is a tie that binds us to our homes, motto on deck of cards showing two dogs chained to a dog house; and on the book's last page and inside back cover this list, the house, the gallery, 4 rooms, red trim, sickness, dinners, sleeptalk, oil lamps, flit can, facing mirrors, our road, up front, back behind, our mule Alice, the fields, Peter, Peter, Peter, the road, the river, the boats, the wake, the railroad, shell roads, the levee, the batture, the cemetery, the tunnel, the bridge, Blue Angels,

Deer Range, Lake Hermitage, cast nets, nutria, armadillo, wild geese, snakes, mink, lizards, cranes, songbirds

from *Incessant Pipe*

Vows

◇　◇　◇

I've been cradling the heavy cat in the half-dark
For an hour
She likes how I make her feel
And I like her—
I was mean to the dog
And now he's dead
Well, not mean
Cold in moments
He could have used the warmth
I could tell and still did nothing about it
And so here I am
Paying—
Which I am accustomed to
And anyhow I am happy
To pay for such horrors, such ill manners
Of my character
Even if I do blame you for it—
How can I empathize with anything
When I can't remember empathy
And you are the only mountain
For miles all around
I've had to learn to be kind again
To uncoil my tendrils into the light
Sometimes I pretend you are not a person
But a stone (how could I love
People again, if I didn't?)

And I warn them: Little Ones,
Don't learn from stones
They are too still
They are too sharp
Sometimes in the moonlight
They whisper terrible things

from Poem-a-Day

What the Dead Can Do

◇　◇　◇

The dead can fly right up to my
window. The dead can be bright
red. The dead can make pictures
come down from walls, and they
can make it so the backyard smells
just like a Christmas tree. The dead

can make a bird land wherever
they want. They can be bright
red if they want. They can make
luck happen, but they can also
make it not. They can curse
your house. They can make

a head of lettuce go bad. They
can wander the streets at night
while I sleep, transmogrify
their tracks sunk in the snow
into those of another mammal.
They can make any song

come on the radio. They can keep
you safe on the road in a whiteout
storm, but they can also not do that.
They can't initiate a rainbow but
if one already comes on the sky
they can add one more.

They hope someone makes
love the way they loved to.
They like visitors at their bones.
Some of them I'm sure
are waiting for their ashes
to be eaten by the young.

from *West Branch*

Gaslighter

◇　◇　◇

A friend makes me a beautiful handbag in all my favorite colors—rusty orange and chocolate polka dots embroidered with golden thread. When I stroll through town, I get a lot of compliments and feel very special. The next day, even though I didn't put anything in the bag, it starts to get heavy. When I bring it back to my friend's house, she turns it upside down and out pours a pyramid of brilliant jewels I have stolen. They are blindingly beautiful! I'm surprised because I don't remember stealing the jewels, but I'm so grateful for the beautiful bag, I give them to her. After a time, the bag becomes heavy again. When my friend empties it, out fall more jewels and a severed hand. I realize it's my hand and start to scream. *There, there,* she says, *you've still got your other hand. Here, let me paint your fingernails a beautiful arctic blue.* She holds my hand in hers with such tenderness I start to cry. *Of course, you're right. Thank you,* I say, and leave with my beautiful bag in my one beautiful hand. Year after year I empty the bag of body parts on her couch, until one day it's too heavy to lift. I drag it down the street by my teeth. *I am hobbled and ugly,* I say to my friend. *No,* she says, *you are a like a rare bird who flies without wings, who sings without a beak. Yes, of course, you're right,* I say. *It's very dark in your house today,* I say, *and I can hardly hear you. I think I'm inside the bag. No,* she says, *you're sitting here right beside me. It's just your head inside the bag and it's beautiful.*

from *Iterant*

Anthony Bourdain

◇ ◇ ◇

The more money we come across
the less tarot we do
the more we chew
in silence
staring
at palm trees
glazed red
on wall tiles
the heads of actual palms
lining the drive-thru
masked with smoke
from burning
Paradise

For a week it's lined our lungs

Driving home I strain to see
the exit signs
and toll booth structures
as the radio
debates ways
to stop the kids
from smoking Juuls
between advertisements
for cleaning solutions
I'll use after
the rains have come

to make our rooms smell
like rooms I've never lived in
which are the rooms
I most prefer

Two months now
we've been married
it feels the same
but different
men stopped mentioning
fucking
the same thing forever
and everyone else
started asking
about the future
sometimes just saying the word
for no reason
I'd compliment the Beaujolais
and then
"in the future you should consider
looking into"
over and over
until the word began
to radiate
in my mind

I find myself
spelling it out
letter by letter
on the roof of
my mouth
while up late folding t-shirts
and now it's two
and I'm beside you in bed
envisioning the ripples
on my Celestial
Sleepytime
Herbal Tea

as I dropped in
my CBD oil
meaning both products
have failed me
once again
and I feel like I
deserve it

For ten years I fell asleep
watching him
wander
Old World cities
and chew
the fattened
parts of animals
but he's been dead since June
now I can't get through
an episode
the future
like a residue
on every frame
how it was there
the whole time
but I failed to see it

We felt like him
we said once
in a foreign country
after a farmer directed us
into a cave
at its end
a secret altar
carved into the limestone
by the once-persecuted
candles burning
in little scooped-out
shelves of rock
a bowl of oil
a vacant space meant
for a holy text

To get there the farmer told us
to walk until we feel like we
should stop then walk
some more and so we did
until the sunglow
of the entrance faded
then disappeared
as we disappeared
in blackness absolute
and stopped
and then you whispered
Can you see me?
No I said
but I know where you are

from *Zyzzyva*

Inaugural

◇　◇　◇

We were told that it is dangerous to touch
And yet we journeyed here, where what we believe
Meets what must be done. You want to see, in spite
Of my mask, my face. We imagine, in time

Of disease, our grandmothers
Whole. We imagine an impossible
America and call one another
A fool for doing so. Can't you feel it? The trouble

With me is I'm just like you. I don't want
To be hopeful if it means I've got to be
Naïve. I've bent so low in my hunger,
My hair's already been in the soup,

And when I speak it's from beneath my self-
Imposed halo. You'll forgive me if you can
Forgive yourself. I forgive you as you build
A museum of weapons we soon visit

To never forget what we once were. I forgive us
Our debts. We were told to wake up grateful,
So we try to fall asleep that way. Where, then,
Shall we put our pains when we want rest?

I don't carry a knife, but I understand
The desperation of those who do,
Which is why I am recounting the facts
As calmly as I can. The year is new,

And we mean to use our imaginations.
One of us wants to raise George Stinney
From the dead. One of us wants a small vial
Of the sweat left on Sylvia Rivera's

Headband. Some want to be the music made
Magical by Bill Withers's stutter.
Others arrive with maps, magnifying
Glasses, and graphite pencils to find

Locations beside the mind where we are not
Patrolled or surveilled or corralled or chained.
I, myself, have come to reclaim the teeth
In George Washington's mouth and plant them

In the backyards of big houses that are not
In my name. My cousins want to share
A single bale of the cotton our mothers
Picked as children. I would love to live

In a country that lets me grow old.
We are otherwise
Easily satisfied. Where do we get
Tangerines for cheap? Can we make it

There on the Metro? How hot is the fire
Fairy blister of chocolate chipotle sauce,
And will you judge me if I taste it? Today,
We've put our hunger down for the time it takes

To come and reconcile ourselves to the land
Because it is holy, to the water
Because it swallowed our ancestors,
To the air because we are dumb enough

To decide on something as difficult
As love. If no one's punishment leads to
Salvation, accountability must be
What waits to mend and move nations.

That's for us to prove. That's the deed
To witness. That's the single item on the agenda
Read in Braille or by eye, ink drying like blood
Spilled this American hour of our lives.

from *The New York Times Magazine*

Proof

◇ ◇ ◇

My body has a legend, he says
mid-story, and wipes his mouth.

Then, as to recite grace,
stands at the table to prove it.

Beneath the drape of his shirt
a savanna of skin ripples slightly.

For a blink, I don't understand
what's missing:

He had no belly button,
his stomach paved mythologically clean.

We'd been so casual
playing catch with origin stories
                        after class
over crepes and pancakes,
our roll call of scars.

We'd been speaking of doctors and mistakes
when his face shifted gears,

he landed his fork like tapping a baton.

This is how boys are. Show
and prove.   Tale of the tape.

People are terrified by skin
       not meeting their expectations.

For years, white women were forbidden
from showing their navels on tv.
The networks were alarmed
                    over what they symbolized,
                    how they seemed to prove something,
       root us together.

Seeing the placenta as nebula
a star-field of skin
a chandelier from which
we're all suspended
flaring out from the same light.

If men can write shame laws over belly buttons

it's no surprise the fumbling
of a Black child
steaming new and helpless
in a cage of fingers.

A rabbit midwifed by a hawk.

              I know this now.

Yet, how I doubted him, Lord.

My sticky, maple fingers trembled in prayer all night.

              from *Alta*

Outer Lands

◇　◇　◇

I'll tell you the story. I was walking
the outer edge of the outer lands

where sporadic signs staked in dunes
warned to keep distant from the mammals;

in fact, there were critical acts in place
to enforce non-molestation,

but between me and the sea
a seal appeared to be having a time of it,

rocked and moaned in a deepening berth
as if trying to summon momentum

to roll down the beach toward water.
In short, it seemed stuck and—it's never far off

in the imagination—dying. I thought
I should bring sea to the seal. I filled

a detergent bottle at the surf and called
the seal "buddy." "You okay, buddy?"

as the tide went this way, then that,
with no sense of intention. An hour before,

I had encountered a friend on this beach,
both of us having walked through our pasts

to that moment. Now he was gone
and I was supposed to be in the mountains

but the mountains were on fire.
From the highway that morning

I watched smoke plumes rise
in each far valley and drove past my exit

straight for the coast, straight into
this story where I gathered

armloads of kelp, making a damp bed
for the seal. Increasingly, my efforts

bore the whiff of not science,
but ritual. I consulted the experts

I wasn't too embarrassed to ask.
On my phone I found a video

of a seal snared in Ocean Shores,
two cops hunched above it, jabbing

at tangled fishing lines with utility knives
as the seal lurched, as the cops jolted

from its teeth. A crowd in sweaters gathered
as the camera narrowed to tattooed flames

on a bicep clenched around the seal.
Beyond this, straggling clouds from Constable

on the horizon, bright light at their edges
reflected in mud. Then one officer

moved toward the SUV, retrieving a club, I feared,
though he returned with a stick and wire loop—

one for the dogs they don't shoot, presumably.
He fastened the catch at the seal's neck

and drove its head into sand until the body stilled,
suddenly submissive. What looked like choking

wasn't—this time—and the line was cut,
and the catch was loosed, and the seal's

arched back bounded for ocean. The algorithm
urged me further: a sea otter pup rescued

by blond hero in board shorts; a stranded whale
in Weymouth; a lone porpoise found

in a British farmer's field fifty miles from
the ocean. Here's the thing: I was looking

at the way things had happened in the world
for evidence of how the world would happen.

Which never works. Each day bears
its crucial variance. And I knew this,

practically had it written on a coffee mug,
but when I was there, and when there

was then, I had to say *stop*—and let red
fill the harbor, and let red wash the shore,

and vow never to touch another living thing
for fear of how my being human might kill it.

from *The Kenyon Review* and *Poetry Daily*

The Innocent

◇　◇　◇

For weeks we watched for hatchlings to come
of three smug eggs tucked into a nest,
the nest tucked into the crook
of a neighbor's honeysuckle. Time nodded,
was nodding—the shred of living, how offhand
the wind teeters toward erosion. Hard at work,
on guard in two backyards, the robins mothered
and fathered their territory daily. And beyond,
our block's alley stretched aimless as fields,
where watching happens by accident,
by nature. They'd squawk on a streetlamp,
a cedar fence, our back stoop, warning off
the tabby, my two young sons, everyone
stuck at home. I lost my mind with watching
and thought it grief or egotism, the bruise
of yesterday, not least the sky
unraveling another season. It was easy
to mistake the bared skeletal pinions
as lawn clippings, old leaves. That circle
in the grass, a massacre of feathers. That
terrible cat. It was easy to lose my mind.
One neighbor said, let's not tell the children,
why know the world as always fated
toward remnant. Another said, go,
take the nest, set it under glass, and make it a lesson.
Instead, I watched our habits pass, the honeysuckle
fade from sickly sweet to nothing but heat.

Call it science. It's summer again, and then
everything's remnant. What did we do those days,
stuck at home, my sons might someday ask. We lived
or tolerated living. We looked away from death.

from *The Believer*

Marriage

◇ ◇ ◇

Of alluvial fields I dreamt.
The idea of marriage:
the great barrier reef with
coral bleached and dying.
Evidence of resilience,
they say, absent a catastrophic
event. Whatever it takes, I've
decided, I don't want
my maternal line to die in me.
I wear my mother's dress.
I watch my body shapeshift.
This face, which hasn't aged
in years, is sunspotted.
I am no movie star. I shrink
from my mother's beauty.
She was, above all else,
good. Her lupus her reward.
Or maybe I am her reward.
I know I'll never be grateful
enough. Between this man
and this man, my eggs are
losing count. Inside your domicile,
how am I to feel alive?
Once again, we face extinction.
The libraries not on fire, but
under dust. I don't believe
in loyalty above happiness.

I dive and dive under
the turbulence. One day, too,
my bones will empty. White blood
cells will mutiny. Do you run
headlong down the hill
into disaster? In the park,
a swarm of gnats insists
on clustering. Insects
claim the interior. The flies
touching my face, again,
again, again, and again.

from *Iterant*

Broken Sestina Reaching for Black Joy

◇　◇　◇

Yesterday I was smashed with the rush of fresh honeysuckle
from the greenway near my house where I walk every day.
I've been trying to write a poem about buried Black bodies
but all I want to write about is Black joy and my pleasure
and Black love and Black lives that don't end with viral death,
so I've stopped consuming the news. I've logged off of social

media for a break. Black bodies are buried in the stickiness of history
every day bodies become the next viral death. And yet, each day
I want to write a poem about pleasure. Black pleasure at the root
instead of viral death. What name now? What Black litany? What
Black elegy is repeated on the news? This cycle: Daunte Wright.
I don't know the details yet, because I can't handle the details yet,
but I am mourning him still. This stanza broke the rules. So, what?

This stanza will break back inside the form of honeycomb to suck
the lyric into compression, reboot restraint, the grief-joy every day
when I walk around Sylvan Park near a broken track of burned Black bodies
but all I want to write about is Black joy and *pleasure pleasure pleasure
please* . . . and Black love and Black lives that don't end with viral death,
so I've stopped consuming the news. I've deleted all my social-media

apps, but logged back in later, saw your name repeating as death
media. Fresh honeysuckle at dusk smells like sweet earth, ripe bodies,
warm floral notes. Heady with romance and nectar. It permeates the day

I walk over the bridge where I often see a single blue heron, not social,
standing stone-still stalking Richland Creek fringed with honeysuckle,
which reminds me of any Mary Oliver poem, such pastoral pleasures.

(I'm also still thinking about Claudia Rankine's blossoming blood
list of Black bodies broken from police brutality inside *Citizen*
on page 134. The memoriam fades into the sheer forecast of names
we know will come.) I picked the sestina for its obsessive listing
and twisting. I selected the sestina to probe a problem I can name
but can't answer. The end words are planets orbiting the math.

Pleasure.
Death.
Honeysuckle
Black bodies.
Social / Media.
Every day.

Every day here are some of the plants and trees I've collected during
my walks. I take pictures on my phone so an app can tell me what they are:
ginkgo, bristly locust, maiden pink, garden star-of-Bethlehem, wild pansy,
birdeye speedwell, eastern redbud, Japanese cherry, apricot, peach,
American holly, beefsteak plant, maypop, common blue wood aster,
calico aster, eastern white pine, southern sugar maple, scarlet morning glory.

Every day I walk past Dutchman's Curve, the eerie site of the Great Train
Wreck of 1918. Deadliest train wreck in American history which killed 101
people, mostly African Americans, headed to a factory to make weapons
for World War I. They were stuffed in rickety wooden cars in the front due
to segregation. The front being the most dangerous spot on a train about
to crash, while white bodies were in steel Pullman cars in the back, protected.

But at 100 mph the wooden cars with Black bodies telescoped, splintered,
and caught fire immediately upon impact with another train on the blind curve.
The historian David Ewing describes bodies writhing in pain. Bodies without heads
and limbs. Bodies unidentified, maimed: "The African Americans that were
on this train did not have a chance to survive, given where they were."

"The cornfield on both sides of the track was trampled by many
feet, and littered with fragments, of iron and wood hurled from the

demolished cars. The dead lay here and there, grotesquely sprawling
where they fell. The dying moaned appeals for aid or, speechless,
rolled their heads from side to side and writhed in agony. Every-
where there was blood and suffering and chaos."
                    —*Tennessean*, June 10, 1918

They asked local butchers to come help manage the gore and horror. Still five
unidentified African American women and three unidentified African American
men destroyed beyond recognition. The railroad masonry abutments remain.
I touched them today.

★   ★   ★

I went on a first date last Thursday. We both leaned into each other's mouths
like two tipped tulips and just kissed each other at a bar called Answer as if that was
an answer—it wasn't. But it was instinctual, sudden and all pleasure. We kissed
all the way down Murphy Road, walking back to our cars, constellation of our juicy
hands everywhere. We kissed and groped, and I stopped obsessively thinking
about death for a few moments, maybe even for a whole evening, which was
the length of a tercet, an envoi sustained
with pleasure reaching for Black desire,
reaching for the transcendence of pain,   if possible. Is it possible?

from *The Atlantic*

Preparing for Sleep

◇　◇　◇

I lie in the dark on my side
thinking about the different
sides that I'm aware of.
The side of a horse.
The side of a ship.
(Old Ironsides.)
A side of beef.
A side of slaw.
Big spoon of mac & cheese
and its subsequent ramekin.
Then ramekin production . . .
the glazing of ramekins . . .
the inspections and the bubble wrap.

I extend one foot out
from under the covers.
The cover of night.
The album's cover.
The barbecue's—its
rustic joie de vivre in
waxed cotton canvas duck.
If it looks like a duck, walks
and quacks like one it
might be a goose.
The goose who crossed the road.
(Why did he do it?)
And later the goose confit.
Meat in its own fat.

A fat lip. A fat knee.
The fatness of cats who
(I retract my foot)
can't fit through the door.
Not just cat doors but any door.
Any door that groans a bit.
Any door that vibrates.
The old door of redemption.
The door of deep feeling.

from *jubilat*

Today: What Is Sexy

◇　◇　◇

Construction worker
with two long French braids,
sexy.

Woman in high-waisted
jeans, white t-shirt,
plain sandals,
sexy.

City sidewalks,
in general.

Breeze,
warm.

Rainbow heart
Pride sticker
on the sidewalk,
sexy.

Having the door
held at the coffee shop.

Tiny portions of food
at the coffee shop,
sexy.

The restraint
cancelling out the lack
of generosity.

The iron gate
around
the dry cleaner's,
sexy.

The black glossy paint,
tipped with fussy,
thornish fleur-de-lis.

The pot of periwinkle
hydrangeas,

huge haphazard
balls of blooms,
sexy.

Woman with gray hair,
tangerine shorts, tan legs,
jay-walking,
sexy.

Two people walking
ahead of me in culottes.

The impulse to react
against skinny jeans.

Dizzy in
the revolving door.

Ducking into the
open green room
to put on mascara.

Green room in low light.
Someone practicing piano
on a dark stage.

Building that holds
the ghosts of dances
choreographed

in basement studios,
sexy.

Suites of offices
on the upper floors,
not.

Stepping into
a crowded
elevator,
no.

And finally,
arriving
at my desk.

That's not
sexy.

But the view
from the window—

the Forbidden River,
calling.

from *Court Green*

Separate but Umbilical Situations Relating to My Father

◇　◇　◇

at nine years old I ran acquainting yourself with this
process is wise he did grandpa before I was able to ask what
he could teach I was chubby with welts and a famous father
who took me out of school to board a bus headed to a
racetrack where I sprained my ankle and was told we'll leave
after the 9th leave cigars that burned cherry-red holes so that
now grown riding my bike from Kmart where they pay me
in cash I am happy to sit below a coat of arms on a
Naugahyde couch counting money in the middle of summer
with a box fan and those times when things happened when
he became afraid the police reported that he'd overdosed at
St. Martha's Church and where have I been when I have been
told so many things because to get out is to still be there and
that means being a woman is unlucky and so I tend to return
to a bird I dreamt of once a mother who said I love him only
I love him with sorrow so please don't search for my father
he is homeless and paid in cash to pick up a broom and sweep

from *West Trestle Review*

Goblin

◇   ◇   ◇

In each of the stories
where children

are led out of their beds
at night by a broken

father or angry stepmother
and marched off

to be fed into the mouth
of a dark wood,

the children are supposed
to die. In some stories

they do. In others they
survive but must kill

a witch or an animal
in order to live

which is, to be fair,
a different kind

of death but a death all
the same. Imagine

the fog around their small
ankles like a shoreline

in the dark. Imagine
how cold their skin

would be beneath the thin
overcoats

of their nightshirts,
the little heat

the parents are giving
off beginning to dissipate

like dew as the children
take that last step

into the copse of trees
and are swallowed up.

There are so many ways
to eat the young.

Yesterday, Owen was riding
his red Radio Flyer

tricycle around and around
our red dining room

table. Get me, poppa,
get me, you're a gob-a-lin,

come get me. And I know
I shouldn't have

really become a goblin,
that that was not what he was

asking for. He wanted his
poppa and a funny voice.

Instead my body grew
like a shadow and turned green,

craven and heavy,
you can't run from the gob-a-lin,

the gob-a-lin, the gob-a-lin,
I sang, and chased him

round the table, you
can't run from the gob-a-lin

I'm going to eat
your skin. Then he stopped,

knowing that I was
no longer there and looked

up at my face and not
seeing my face began to cry

and shake. I knelt down
and held him,

and said I'm sorry
it's just poppa,

was that too scary? We
won't play that anymore and he

calmed a little and said
I don't want him

poppa,
tell the gob-a-lin not to

come back. When you ask
parents how they ever raised

their children they will
often say

half the time I had no idea
what I was doing.

But I think we do know
what we are doing. And so does

the forest, and the dark
in the forest,

and the wind in the dark,
and the beasts,

the broken fathers, the angry
stepmothers,

the unconditional bond
become errant.

from *The American Poetry Review*

TISHANI DOSHI

Advice for Pliny the Elder, Big Daddy of Mansplainers

◇   ◇   ◇

Great Man, now that you are dead, allow me to squeeze your hand. The sage
bushes in Umbria are heavy with bees, so I'm killing them with hypnosis. I
am a mere woman—inferior lettuce—but I understand swoon aka *mirabilia*.
I fill this cup with nectar and offer it to soothe your Vesuvian wounds. I share
your love of baths and classification and sure, if we have to point to a god in the
sky, why not call him Thunderbolt? I too believe sewers are *the* great architectural
invention. I do all my searching on roads. It has been two thousand years, so we
can forgive some of your assertions. The sea mouse who helps whales find their
way by parting the brows above their eyes. The one-eyed humans and sciapods
with umbrella feet, the whole exotic bestiary. If I had no mouth but could live
off the smell of apples I'd move to Kashmir—scratch that, maybe Sussex.
Once a month, when the blood comes, I go out to lie in whatever field I
find to feel the scorch rise and the crops wither. Our powers are much
depleted. I can stand among men in full swing of my *menstruus* and
nothing will dim their ability to tell me about me. There are birds
I can't name at the window this morning and dogs in the valley
beyond, who are using their bell-shaped lungs to announce
their happiness again and again and again. Nothing has
changed. We worry about the wane and winnow. In
your time perhaps the ladies used bits of cut-up
smocks but these days we have menstrual cups.
Desire is still a kind of ruin—that silly bird
fluttering against the window net,
trying to get in, the body's steady
lilt toward oblivion. They say you
had a sister, like Shakespeare's—

mostly overlooked. That it was she
who first noticed the smoky clouds
that sent you on your way. Dear
Pliny, I guess you never heard the
one about curiosity. The cat is real.
The earth never tires of giving
birth. If you get too close
to a volcano, you should
know it may erupt.

from *The New York Review of Books*

Let Me

◇　◇　◇

Let me tell you, America, this one last thing.

I will never be finished dreaming about you.

I had a lover once. If you could call him that.

I drove to his apartment in a faraway town,

like the lost bear who wandered to our cul-de-sac

that summer smoke from the burning mountain

altered our air. I don't know what became of her.

I drove to so many apartments in the day.

America, this is really the very last thing.

He'd stocked up, for our weekend together,

on food he knew I would like. Vegetarian

pad Thai, some black-bean-and-sweet-potato chili,

coconut ice cream, a bag of caramel popcorn.

Loads of Malbec. He wanted to make me happy,

but he drank until I would have been a fool

not to be afraid. I'd been drinking plenty, too.

It was too late to drive myself anywhere safe.

I watched him finger a brick as if to throw it

at my head. Maybe that's a metaphor. Maybe

that's what happened. America, sometimes it's hard

to tell the difference with you. All I could do

was lock myself inside his small bedroom. I pushed

a chest against the door and listened as he threw

his body at the wood. Listened as he tore apart

the pillow I had sewn him. He'd been good to me,

but this was like waiting for the walls to ignite.

You've heard that, America? In a firestorm

most houses burn from the inside out. An ember

caught in the eaves, wormed through the chinking, will flare up

in the insulation, on the frame, until everything

in the house succumbs to the blaze. In the morning,

I found him on the couch. Legs too long, arms spilling

to the carpet, knuckles bruised in the same pattern

as a hole in the drywall. Every wine bottle

empty. Each container of food opened, eaten,

or destroyed. "I didn't want you to have this,"

he whispered. If he could not consume my body,

the food he'd given me to eat would have to do.

Have you ever seen a person walk through the ruins

of a burnt-out home? Please believe me, I am not

making light of such suffering, America.

Maybe the dream I still can't get over is that,

so far, I have made it out alive.

from *The New Yorker*

Ode to Sudanese Americans

◊ ◊ ◊

basma & rudy were first   each holding
    a mirror in her arms   where i could see
my face as their faces   & we pierced

our noses & wore gamar boba
    in our ears & everyone at the party
thought them hoop earrings   & in the new york years

i crowd smoky bars alongside ladin
    & shadin & majid & linda & nedal
atheel & amir & elkhair   & mo & mohammed & mo

& we are forever removing our shoes in each other's
    apartments   ashing cigarettes
into the incense burner   making tea

with the good dried mint our mothers taught us
    to keep in the freezer   next to the chili
powder from home   making songs & dinner

& jokes in our parents' accents   & i am funniest
    when i have two languages to cocktail
when i can say *remember* & everyone was there

the rented room at the middle school on sundays
    where our parents volunteered to teach us arabic
to watch us bleat   alef baa taa thaa   & text

our american boyfriends that we were bored
     & at restaurants everyone asks if we are related
& we say yes   we do not date because we are probably

cousins   we throw rent parties & project the video
     where albalabil sing gitar alshoug & i am not
the only one crying   not the only one made & remade

by longing   the mutation that arabic makes of my english
     metallic noises the english makes in my arabic
we ululate at each other's weddings   we ululate at the club

& sarah & hana make the mulah vegan   & in english safia
     spells her name like mine but pronounces it
like *purified*   sews a patch of garmasees

to the back of my denim jacket   we wash our underwear
     in the sink & make group texts on whatsapp
we go home & take pictures of the pyramids

we go home & take pictures of the nile   we move
     to other cities & feel doubly diasporic
& your cousin's coworker's little sister emails me

a list of bigalas in oakland   brings me crates
     of canned fava beans from her own parents'
basement   & i say sudanese american & mean also

british sudanese   & canadian & australian & raised
     in the gulf   azza & yousra & amani & yassmin
& it's true that my people are everywhere

the uncles driving taxis at the end of our nights
     the pharmacist who fills my prescription
who is named for the mole denoting beauty

adorning her left cheek   guardian spirits of my every
     hookah bar   of my every untagged photograph
of crop tops & short shorts   & pierced cartilage & tattoos

of henna & headscarves & undercuts & shaved heads
my tapestries   embroidered with hundreds
of little mirrors   glinting like sequins in the changing light

from Poem-a-Day

A Bulldozer's American Dream

◇ ◇ ◇

At the construction site the bulldozer works
days & nights. No, it is the man inside who works.
The man & his machine are one. After the stars
& dogs & coffees brewed with hands of his loved one,
her night hair of soft river, of his own volition
the man chose to participate in this heavy-lifting labor.
Wrong, it's the machine that does. No more
than twenty-five: the man, forearm knotted, grips
the handle & the machine's hydraulic stick follows—
An extension of his body & to that extent, his mind.
His mind, as we know it, does not want to be a man,
or anything with a preconceived structure.
But how can he resist this pleasure, his thighs
harvesting, his glazed nape taut as a stag's skin,
discharging summer rain. It is the mind that cannot
resist this sweet perk of the earth. It is the mind
that tames the bulldozer's tender monstrosity & orders
it to pick up, with connivance, those dusk-damaged
bones for its master & dig into the deep-delved
darkness, an interior otherwise unattainable.
Some evenings, the man leaves the construction site
for steaks & candles & wine thick as plagued blood,
musing the neck of his wife, whose good flesh
is continuous as his dreams in which the earth
will never betray him, for he is its filial son,
competent at his duty: *Fill the earth & subdue it.*

Then the machine, without its master, lowers its bucket
in rain. Then through the hard latticework of this city,
its metal drilled by a known silence. It hurts to look at it.
A sad thing. The machine still is not a part of anything.

from *Guernica*

1965: Harriet Richardson Wipes Galway Kinnell's Face after State Troopers Beat Him with a Billy Club

◇ ◇ ◇

for Matthew

In Selma that day. The photograph. It is the way she is looking at him. Not his name. His pallor. Not the city, nor the event, not even the blood on his neck. When I saw the picture I realized someone cared enough to take it. There was only one lens. Then, the entire world wasn't always watching. She pressed that cloth to his neck as intimate as a kiss whispered into the channel of an ear. Spontaneously. Sudden and overwhelming as a father's embrace after a father's failure to embrace. I was two years old. It was before I knew what I was born into. It would have been illegal for me to have married my husband. My husband stares at the picture, but a man so compassionate cannot easily take in its lack. It takes the violating or the violated to know. You know why Galway was there. Why pretend? The reward of courage is this: my husband told his parents he would marry me. Period. He expected his parents to live up to the values they espoused. They have. If I cry, my blue-eyed father-in-law—whose father left Germany in the nascent rise of Hitler—cries. Galway's eye to Harriet's brown as mine. Look at the way he looks at her. Like a sun rising twice to be Galway that day, looking up in the face of the tender after terror. See, the grace of gratitude. He being there. She being her.

from *The Kenyon Review*

Sea: Night Surfing in Bolinas

◇　◇　◇

Maybe enough light • to score a wave • reflecting moonlight, sand • reflecting
moonlight and you • spotting from shore • what you see only • as silhouette against
detonating bands • of blue-white effervescence • when the crown of the falling •
swell explodes upward • as the underwave blows through it • a flash of visibility quickly
• snuffed by night • the surf fizzling and churning • remitting itself to darkness •
with a violent stertor • in competition with no other sounds

paddling through dicey backwash • the break zone of • waist-high NW swell •
as into a wall of obsidian • indistinguishable from night sky • diving under, paddling fast
• and before I sit • one arm over my board • I duck and • listen a moment
underwater • to the alien soundscape • not daytime's clicks and whines of • ship
engines and sonar • but a low-spectrum hum • the acoustic signature of fish, squid, •
crustaceans rising en masse • to feed at the surface I feel • an eerie peacefulness veined
with fear

after twenty minutes the eyes • adjust, behind the hand dragging through water •
bioluminescent trails • not enough light • to spot boils • or flaws in nearing •
waves appear even larger • closing-in fast • then five short strokes into a dimensionless
• peeler, two S-shaped turns, the • kick out, and from shore • your shout

it is cowardice that turns my eyes • from the now-empty beach • for with you I
became • aware of an exceptional chance • I don't believe in • objective description,
only • this mess, experience, the perceived • world sometimes shared • in which life
doesn't • endure, only • the void endures • but your vitality stirred it • leaving
trails of excitation • I've risen from the bottom of • myself to find • I exist in you
• exist in me and • against odds I've known even rapture, • rare event, • which
calls for • but one witness

from *The Paris Review*

Second Wind

◇   ◇   ◇

I think this is my second wind,
my sister said. Very
like the first, but that
ended, I remember. Oh
what a wind it was, so powerful
the leaves fell off the trees.
I don't think so,
I said. Well, they were
on the ground, my sister said. Remember
running around the park in Cedarhurst,
jumping on the piles, destroying them?
You never jumped, my mother said.
You were good girls; you stayed where I put you.
Not in our heads,
my sister said. I put
my arms around her. What
a brave sister you are,
I said.

from *The Threepenny Review*

APRIL GOLDMAN

Into the Mountains

◇　◇　◇

When I imagine the dead I think of them doing absolutely nothing. Every morning
a tiny red ant
has left bites up my arm. I'm not god

as far as I know, though it's possible. Mostly I feel like a child or elder, or a thing scraped
together from what's in between.

One wants the blue indifference of the ocean to get inside them. One wants it to stay there
and curl up.

Everyone dreams, my therapist says, of leaving their car on the shoulder to disappear
into the mountains forever. This is normal.
　　　　It's as normal as rain. A metaphor for how faultless the earth is, a kind of enveloping.

I crinkle like tinfoil when I laugh. The bees vituperate the wind, tiny purple lupine. I wish
　　to look
at my great body
for long hours in the mirror, my body which is itself long.

This poem is over now. This poem smells like something buried a while.

When I think of the dead, I think of this poem. It has thought and felt, fallen in love,
dipped its feet in cold water,
crunched through piles of leaves. Now it is time.

My favorite word is *if*. I have a favorite word. I have a favorite everything.

I have a favorite part of my body. It's my mom. Mom, I say. Mom mom mom mom. Sing to me as you carry me away.

from *Ploughshares*

Theories of Revenge

◇   ◇   ◇

I think about the man who must be dead
by now and his undifferentiated son
and how they sat beside one another
that morning I nearly died in their yard.
I never learned his name, hair color,
where he went to church if he did,
and this morning I'm thinking
about the ethics of giving him a minor limp.
Some old wound that healed
wrong in another life. Tendon
that snapped in a filthy alley in San Juan.
1967. The light was different,
then, because the sun was.
Everything was. Years before my birth.
Years before Elvis died
on the toilet, his body ruined and ruptured,
and even though I grew up
in Tennessee I've never been to Graceland.
There is so much in life to regret.
To desire unto pain. To ignore, also.
There I lay in the weeds
of the ditch like garbage,
my body harmed forever,
though nobody then would really believe it,
and I felt little: some ache,
but mostly nothing, a spooky lack of weight
on the summer-hot ground.

I think there was panic
in the air above me like a ghost
and I struggled to breathe.
Do not move me or pick me up or touch me,
I begged the old man.
Something is wrong. Something was
wrong with the bicycle
and now inside me was something terrible
and lasting and final
and I think I wanted it all to be a bad dream.
The way my head fell over
when they stood me up. The horror when I collapsed.
There was no blood anywhere.
No visible wound. Just a boy in yellow surrounded by strangers.

from *The Missouri Review*

The Life of a Writer

◇　◇　◇

the life of a writer is desire
　　　i hammer into the page
　　　　　　i make up my mind: the streetlight

is not the moon, but anything can be
　　　made beautiful under the ease
　　　　　　of my hammer

i wish you could see that i write in blue ink
　　　the color of oceans & early mornings
　　　　　　& everything is clear like

tears rushing toward the chin
　　　of my desire. i pen what i'm meant
　　　　　　to pen. how deep in love i am

& how silly of me to spend all morning dreaming
　　　about love & not expect my
　　　　　　desire to set me free

the knives of my fingers tap
　　　out the notion that if i turn the key
　　　　　　it will unlock.

admittedly, i am foolish
　　　about love—a simple *yes* excites me—
　　　　　　'cause i know that all that i require will be met

like water meets the tongue. it's scary
       desire, a small fan at my window in the summer,
          a booklight lighting the pages of my life.

from Poem-a-Day

What Would You Ask the Artist?

◇　◇　◇

I. DIY SESTINA

DEAR	SIR		BLUE	I
HELLO	MASTER		SKY	US
ESTEEMED	PAINTER	HOW DID YOU MAKE	DUSK	WE
GODISH	GHOST		DENIM	IT
IF I MAY	MATTISE		RAIN	THEM
G.O.A.T.	HENRI		SAPPHIRE	YOU

WHAT WOULD YOU ASK THE ARTIST ABOUT THE PAINTING?

II. EPISTOLARY SESTINA

Dear Painter, can you share how you made the blue we
Find in certain of your paintings? Sometimes I catch it
Throwing a Godish glow over everything in the eye
Of a storm covered in lightning. I fear without you
The color will not be seen again except perhaps inside us
Where the bones hold its mercurial shades in them.

Matisse, Sir, did your brushes have the blues in them?
Where else might the remains be found? We
Sometimes find the color in denim when rain dampens it.

61

Once or twice making love when I closed my eyes
I found myself in a tabernacle of the hue you
Have left hanging on the walls around us.

Hello G.O.A.T., Master of the Show, I have very little use
For blueberries, blue jays, skies, sapphire, & the hems
In the garments of policemen, but the lines we
See hand-painted on porcelain come close. I might use it
On a Ming vase or in cases of chaos or rapture & if I
Fell into darkness, I would gaze upon it & thank you.

Mid-fall, Icarus shows how a misstep expands behind you,
How one can come to a conclusion using the wrong calculus.
The man who covered his coins in honey before eating them
In "Gooseberries" also turned a distasteful blue. The ennui we
Wish to cover & uncover & free & contain. As in how hard it
Is to describe your own accent. As in the way *The Bluest Eye*

Has so much blackness in it. If people born in a season of ice
Are usually crawling by summer, how much do you
Suppose that determines their general disposition? Above us
Are constellations a soul needs for guidance, the anthems
Of sawdust & approximation. As if in matters of our bodies we
Are the least reliable witnesses. You find upon exit

The tubes of desuetude painters used in the exhibit.
I was born for this moment because this is the moment I
Was born, you say. It is always the color of history. Can you
Share how you made the blues outlast & outline us?
How long did you swim or drown or float or swallow them,
Esteemed Ghost, Henri, if I may, ennui, Henri, ennui?

III. ENVOY OF PICASSO'S BLUE

The first drawing Pablo Picasso made as a toddler
Dragging a single blue crayon across a sheet of onionskin,
Made his father, an average painter, weep with desire

And weep again showing the drawing to Picasso's mother
Who also wept. The drawing was said to have been lost
After the death of Picasso's sister, Conchita, of diphtheria

When the family moved to Barcelona, but it
Reappeared years later somewhere you'd never expect.
To truly grasp any of Picasso's later work you should know

Whether the sister's death conjured a bird & bull's
Eye view of loss & faith & if the experience
Instilled a constant mysterious feeling in Picasso,

Whether everything that happens to the artist before
Age nine or ten or even before 9 or 10 a.m. influences
Whether an instrument is held like a tool or weapon

Some days. Loss & desire is always in the eye
Of the maker & beholder. Picasso, of course, grew
To make many more haunted, perceptive scenes,

But the stranger who found the drawing had no idea
Who'd made it, only that the lines in blue crayon
On onion paper conjured a mysterious feeling in him.

It looks somehow like a perfectly drawn landscape,
Said the neighbor, resting his wiry hand
On the fence & thinking the stranger showing him

A drawing in the middle of the day slightly stranger
Than he'd thought before. Returning to his work
when the stranger left, the neighbor felt something

Like a quixotic quaking in his blind spots. He spent
the rest of his days trying to describe the feeling.
It was a depiction of the body's geometries, the eye doctor

Replied when the stranger asked his opinion. He sent
The stranger home after an inconclusive eye exam & then
Went home to bed himself. The doctor closed his eyes

Around his tears & slept for six or seven days, dreaming
Of nudes posing before a surgeon with a palette knife.
When the stranger got home & showed the drawing

To his wife, she said it was clearly a portrayal of liberty.
The artist marking the presence of God, she explained,
Pausing over the thickest of the lines, "and asking why

And which paths will conjure the opposite of faith
And time." Her hair, the stranger noticed, was no longer
As it was when she was his bride. "Blind spots always leave

A stain," the wife said after dinner, though the stranger
Had long put the drawing away. She kept trying to describe
What she'd seen. How not to disappear completely,

She said, lying in bed while her husband, the stranger,
Saw the drawing burning in a nightmare. It was clearly a tale
About slaves. The artist was suffering a notion of color.

The wife cried herself to sleep that night & dreamed
She was being covered in waves of saltwater & gold,
The ephemera of souls lost between African & American

Shores, a blue between the sky & shark parlor,
Lovely as the most lovely of the sisters to leap
Into the waters & live free as the bride of the sea.

from *The Georgia Review*

:::[to the voice of the age]:::

◇ ◇ ◇

They gave up their fear of sincerity

They gave up   their decorated nights

Evening birdsong had folded into chalk

Evening shadows grew less white

> We'd been faithful mostly
> to our own special tribe

Couldn't keep the burned forests alive

Of the beasts of the apocalypse   one was light green

It was a dream   We didn't choose that

We chose the rat   the cat   the fox   the past

& when we sang to ourselves   the song went

What is the voice of the age my friends
What is the age of the voice
   Adenine   Cytosine   Guanine   Uracil
The voice of the age is a fragment

O sea of glass   Cart of straws   O air

round as the love of moths

Hard to forgive certain centuries my friends

The age of the voice is the choices
The voice of the page is the voices

O love song in an old blue cart

Wheel of ciphers   wheel of eyes
Wheel of beauty code & blues
The voice of the age is the voices

4-22-20   2,590,125
7-31-20   17,321,394
for GGOB

from *Alta*

Against Death

◇   ◇   ◇

After my best friend died I became jealous of the fireflies and kept smashing them against my forehead. I wanted my loneliness to be visible to those I loved. For people to see the yellow balloons I hid in my lungs. What I'm saying is I couldn't breathe for an entire year. When they tore down her elementary school, we all lined up, days later, for bricks. We held them against our bodies. I'd like to think this is how we embrace our ghosts. Years later, it took my grandfather three days to die. I grew so bored I left to get ice cream. In the car, with the July sun soaking my back, I let my tongue protest death. Hours after my grandfather died, I wanted to take a photo of his body. His skin the color of faded marigolds. As a child, when my goldfish died I mourned the entire ocean. My father told me *children in Palestine die every day*. Hours before dying from cancer, Jim said *take care of yourself*. I said *you too*. When I visit graveyards now, all I see is grass and grass and grass. I think about how it takes forever to get to nowhere. Maybe I've outlived my life. And would like to become a bird. Dear God. Dear Earth. Dear Clouds. Why should anything die? I want it all to live forever. What I mean is I want to stand in my garden and gaze at the sunflowers. Amen.

from *TriQuarterly*

Ode to Everything

◇ ◇ ◇

Somehow, I have never thought
to thank the ice cream cone
for building a paradise in my mouth,
and can you believe I have never
thought to thank the purple trout lily
for demonstrating its six-petaled dive
or the yellow circle in a traffic light
for illustrating patience. My bad.
In my life, I have failed to praise
the postman whose loyalty is epic,
the laundress who treasures my skinny jeans
and other garments, and the auto repairman
who clangs a wrench inside my car tightening
her own music. Were my name called and I
were summoned on a brightly lit stage to accept
a little statuette, after staring in utter
disbelief, I would thank my dentist
as well as my neighbor who sits vigil
beside the dying far away from the lights,
and my fourth-grade teacher who brought
down three-taped rulers on my hands
as punishment for daydreaming out a window
during an exam I already completed. Mea culpa.
Now that I know the value of the peaks
across from Flanders Hill, I will forever express
reverence for their green crowns.

I will never fail again to say small devotions for
the scar on a friend's face that lengthens
when I walk into a room.

from *Northwest Review*

Capitalism

◇ ◇ ◇

the best thing I can do for my momma is stay out her pocket
this gets truer the older I get but it's been true since I got here
at the grocery store check out I suck my teeth and curse the air
what the hell did I buy my voice almost as sharp as my mother's
except everything in this cart's for me   I pick up my privilege
and push past her shadow where she still stands scouring the receipt for error
double scan   a missed discount   the usual trickery
in high school when they ask what I want to do when I grow up
I say *not starve* and mean it   I don't dream of excess or labor
my momma works hard her daddy worked hard
all my ancestors were worked hard   in boston the white teacher
at the white school in the white neighborhood where the black women hold
the little white hands of bright eyed blonde children like work visas
looks dead in my face and says her grandfather worked hard
and that's why we have that house on martha's vineyard
in her wedding photos she smiles in her ivory dress
with her ivory beaux and the white pillars
of her grandfather's white house rise up to frame them

from *The Rumpus*

How Much I Loved This Life

◇　◇　◇

I lay in the dark afraid of the dark,
Once, in Alabama, in 1954,
The year before electricity,
And prayed and could not pray

One lamp for all the world
And, listening, heard the L&N
Screech at Lacon, and then
The unmuted spirit breathing of the house.

I lay in the dark afraid of the dark
And thought of the word eternity
And of the hydrogen bomb.
Sometimes now in sleep I ululate.

When Katy shakes me, asking why,
I mean to keep things light. I say,
"That is the noise I always make
When I am being devoured."

from *Literary Matters*

LAURA KASISCHKE

When a bolt of lightning falls in love

◊ ◊ ◊

with an old woman, sex is reinvented
as the world's first toaster oven.

When lightning falls in love with a middle-
aged woman, lightning gives

birth to an electric guitar. When
lightning falls in love

with a married man, his wife becomes
an arsonist. When lightning falls

in love with an arsonist, she
gives birth to a son. When

lightning falls in love with my son, I wake up
to the streaking comet-scream of the fire alarm

in the hallway of a motel
on the wrong side of an ocean, and

I think, Thank God. I think: all
this lightning has always had

a plan, and if lightning can make plans, and if
lightning, like lightning's plans, go on, and

will go on
after I've gone—then

my own lightning's work here is almost done.

from *The Georgia Review*

LAURA KOLBE

Buried Abecedary
for Intensive Care

◇　◇　◇

It's called an awakening trial when the pleasanter drugs stop. It's
called bucking when the lungs and vent jam wind against each other.
It's called clubbing when the fingernails thicken to spoons from lack
of oxygen. It's called drug fever when no one knows why. It's called
elevation when the eyes can see where the feet should be. It's called
fasting when radiology foretells like a speaking goat on the blood-
blue mountain. It's called gunk when they suction the trach. It's
called HIPAA when no one tells. It's called inspiration just before the
triggered cough. It's called jaw thrust when the head is prepared for the
Macintosh blade. It's called kin when they don't shy speechless from
the gunk. And when they do. It's called labored when breath outmoans
machines. It's called manual blood pressure when you hope the
machine lied. It's called nitroprusside when the body is flushed like a
cinema. It's called octreotide when the blood untucks the napkin of the
diner. It's called a pan scan when the body won't tell. It's called a query
when insurer and the bank won't tell. Called resuscitation but it isn't.
Called shock when it started as resuscitation. Called Trendelenburg
when the feet are in the air. Called underventilation when the gas is
more like the future planet's. Called the vagus nerve when touching
the neck makes the rhythm stop. Called weaning when the fentanyl
hangs salivary at the chin of the bed. Called xeroform when the gauze
smells like gin and tonic. Called you when it's a question of error.
Called zeroing out when they reset the machines for the next body.

from *The New York Times Magazine*

74

The Rest Is Silence

◊ ◊ ◊

I've been sitting at this window in MiKro
for the past hour and a half on a Friday afternoon

in Hamden, watching folks come in to start
their weekends, and every single one of them

has been White. I came here to unwind
after a phone interview a few colleagues and I

conducted with three job candidates,
all White. I was the only one participating not

White. All of the other seven finalists
the other subcommittees are interviewing

are White. All of the other subcommittee profs
are White. We will likely hire three new

White profs to join a department in which all
but one of its fourteen full-time profs (hi)

are White. At no point will we talk, unless I
bring it up, about the problem of adding

three new White profs to this all but all-White
department, because our job applicant pool

(according to HR) yielded a 7% diversity rating,
3% below the national average but deemed

"acceptable." There were 93 candidates, so six,
maybe seven people of color self-identified.

In my advanced poetry workshop this semester,
every student is White. In my intro to poetry course,

17 out of 18 are White. These percentages
are typical. They've been so since I started here

in 2012. They are, apparently, "acceptable."
Less than 7% diversity. When I got to this bar,

not many people were here, I was feeling good,
I like the hickory-smoked chicken wings, locally

brewed IPAs, but as one by one every new White
person filed in, I felt myself shrinking into a tinier

%, becoming more and more miKroscopic.
I'm not surprised. I've been to this bar many times,

it's my favorite bar in Hamden, I like to come here
after work to have a beer and work on things

before hitting the road back home to Brooklyn.
Always it is all White except for me—it's like

our thing. Mind you, not almost all White, *all* White.
6:30 now and the happy-hour weekend crowd

is pouring in, the place is packed, I look up
and watch every new White customer walk in

with a peculiar, dangerous sort of pleasure,
like I'm itching a rash. I'm lucky this doesn't

bother me that much, I know when I come here
I'm going to leave and drive back home to Brooklyn.

But imagine if I lived here. When people at my school,
students and faculty alike, ask me why I don't

live here, why I commute an hour and a half
from Brooklyn, they don't understand how this

is a racist question. Imagine if I told them that.
Man, how can you bear that commute?

Man, how can you bear that racist question?
Look around you in this bar. Look at every single

person walking through that door. Let's count
how many people look like me by the end

of the night. Do you ever do that obligatory
room check, turning to scan the faces around you

to see how many non-White ones there are? No?
Well maybe don't ask me about my commute then.

It's that never having occurred to you that this room
might be a problem, might make some people

uncomfortable, might make them, consciously
or unconsciously, change their behavior, their very

personality, that reveals your racist blindness—
no, that's not the right word, it's too strong,

ableist, suggests there's something wrong
with you, some flaw, whereas you don't think

there's anything wrong, it's a racist innocence.
And you're not wrong, what's so bad about

what's happening here? Are these bad people?
Is anyone saying some racist shit or not serving me

or causing me physical harm? Am I not being
included like everyone else, am I not being

treated equally? I couldn't call you a *racist*.
You're not *doing* anything. I would never tell

you to your face you're asking me a racist question
or explain you're enjoying a racist innocence

(except in this poem), I wouldn't want to do that
to you, you're too innocent, it's not your fault,

I'd immediately feel like an asshole. And that's
the problem, isn't it, innocent? You go on innocent,

places like this go on innocently looking this way.
What's the bar supposed to do, institute some kind

of diversity quota? It's a business, these are the people
who live here, these are its customers, it needs

to make money, there's nothing racist about that.
Right? It's not turning people of color away or not

serving them, the people who work here are all
nice, I've never had a problem other than seeing

White person after White person walk in without
interruption, which is not against the law, maybe

I'm just a whiner, overly sensitive, I don't have
to drink here, I don't even live here, what's the bar

supposed to do, offer free beer to people of color?
Host People of Color Night? That would be absurd.

Right? Hire more people of color to change
the complexion of the room and attract more

customers of color? That would be against the law,
potentially, if it were found the bar hired POC

over more qualified White candidates, and let's be
real, how many POC work in the craft beer industry?

Compared to White folks? Especially in this area?
You'd have to go out of your way to find someone

when there are all these super-qualified White folks
already available to hire. And they're all so nice,

hardworking, experienced, most importantly
they love beer, they're passionate about it,

it's the one thing in their life they care about
the most, they'd fit right in here, they'd hit

the ground running, whereas a person of color . . .
would they even be happy? Would they want

to stay? Wouldn't they have other interests,
aspirations? This job is not easy. It's mostly grunt

work, a person with aspirations might find it
difficult to endure, especially if they already feel

out of place. All of this reasoning makes sense
even as I sit here feeling more miKroscopic

sipping my white beer. What's funny is how absurd
diversity initiatives seem at a bar that do not

at a university, offering free beer to bring POC
into this space seems hilarious in the imagination,

especially when I picture furious White customers,
whereas offering financial aid at a university

does not. What's funny is what's not so funny,
how diversity initiatives at a bar only seem absurd

because not enough people are talking about them
to give them traction, admitting POC or women

into a university let alone giving them financial aid
seemed as absurd if not more so to White gents

not so long ago. And by absurd I mean so against
the natural, historical inertia of the norm

as to seem like a physical violation, that inertia
is the bedrock of all true power, the saturation

of the same so-be-it that has always been, what makes
a 7% diversity rating "acceptable," what can we do

about it, these are the people who applied,
we don't know how many of them self-identified,

this is our demographic, it's not our fault
POC are not taking advantage of this opportunity,

we made it available to everyone, what are we
supposed to do, redo the whole job search?

Change the qualifications? Cast a wider net
with our advertising? Change the whole way

we do business? Who's going to do all that work
and spend all that money? You? Of course not

me, I'm not in charge here, if I were, the whole
business would be built differently from

the ground up, inclusivity and diversity
would be part of the very fabric of how we do

things, we wouldn't need to pay for outside
assessment of our diversity or hire a Chief

Diversity Officer or construct a strategic plan
for increasing diversity, a plan that slyly gives

a company convenient cover if anyone
should point out the factual lack of diversity

among their ranks and the problems arising
because of that, now there's official language

"proving" the company takes diversity seriously
and is doing something about it, a simulacrum

of diversity including a definition that expands
its meaning beyond race and gender to include

class, ability, sexuality, age, religion, education
and pretty much anything under the sun,

so that looked at this way, diversity has already
been achieved, there's no need to do anything

despite what the strategic plan seems to suggest
by its existence, if not by what it actually says,

the company brilliantly grows so inclusive
by the letter of its own law as to become more

exclusive, as now White job committees can
hire more White employees to entrench their own

"diversity." There is a "yesterday I find almost
impossible to lift," as Elizabeth Bishop said

at the end of her career, not talking about race,
but I feel it mid-career, or perhaps pre-career,

as whatever career I have always feels like a prelude
to an actual one, and this because of race,

I can say something about our lack of diversity
to my department, how for us and our school

this starts with race, as we don't have a gender
issue and race is the most easily visible form

of diversity missing here, making any POC
uncomfortable and strangely causing even more

discomfort to White folks when the subject
is brought up, they won't go out of their way

to increase racial diversity but they'll go out
of their way to talk about this problem, acting

like they want to do something, saying,
"We need to have a conversation about this,"

then having meeting after meeting
where talk replaces action and postpones

the problem for another meeting, but will talk
of any kind change the room around me?

Look at where I'm sitting. Imagine me
saying something. What would the reaction be?

Who would I say something *to*? Another
customer? The bartender? The manager?

The owner? Where would I even start?
At least at a university there's some kind

of intellectual and political context for what
I'd like to say, but at a bar? On a Friday night?

There might be some talk here and there
about the problems of race in America,

but no one wants to hear that the problem
is them, especially on a Friday night, what did

they do, they're just trying to kick back
and have a good time. And truthfully I don't

think they are the problem, the problem
starts so far in back of us, in all the yesterdays

that have built up this room and others
like it without question, there's no moving

the massive weight of them without total
cataclysm, or by tiny, incremental, all but

imperceptible shifts that feel like waiting,
or doing nothing, so saying something

feels, in the end (because there is no end),
like silence, except now you're full of unrest

.

because you've caused unrest, you've ruined
everyone's happy hour, starting with your own—

I just want to sit here after work and eat
these hickory-smoked chicken wings and drink

these locally brewed IPAs, not so ruefully aware
of how doing so participates in and bankrolls

this hand-crafted Whiteness, how my tastes,
which feel so particular to me, are informed

by Whiteness, Whiteness of a certain kind
that I perceive as cool and try to embody

with my own Asian slant, this bar, I know,
appeals to me because it looks and feels like

Brooklyn, starting with it being housed
in a renovated historic building (or at least

what looks like such a building), the name
is Korny but this is the closest you're gonna get

to Brooklyn in Hamden, I recognize all
the Brooklyn design touches, how Brooklyn

itself is an import for any place trying
to commodify its local, historic identity,

and this is a White Brooklyn, I'm such
a sucker for it, much as I say I'm becoming

uncomfortable with all the White people
walking in, obviously I feel more comfortable

here than anywhere else in Hamden, I keep
coming here though this keeps happening,

something about this place feels inclusive,
or inclusive enough to keep me consuming

rather than speaking out about its problems,
except in the space of this poem, and let's face it,

a poem is a more acceptable way of breaking
silence, it can be ignored (especially one this long)

and doesn't ruin anybody's happy hour, in fact
it goes well with happy hour if read for some

indie reading series at your neighborhood bar,
I can even see it working here, though there

might be some initial discomfort, everyone
likes to be challenged politically and made

uncomfortably aware of our nation's problems
when there's a time limit, booze and packaging

as art and entertainment, it's a good discussion
starter, "edgy," an edifying hors d'oeuvre

to clear the conscience before the evening's
inanities, and I'm not *too* angry, which helps,

look at how I've already qualified my complaints
by showing how I'm complicit in everything

I'm complaining about, reassuring Whiteness
that there's no real problem here, everyone

can go back to their drinks, plus I'm Asian
American, White folks don't find my kind

(that) threatening anymore, at least not since
Executive Order 9066, I might not feel I fit in

but I fit in, Asian American is the new White,
or the closest to White of any POC, which I

find troubling, to say the least, how many
times do you see a room full of White people

and the only or the most POC present
are Asian? I almost wonder if we even count

anymore, I see this so often, I only don't see it
here because *I'm that one present*, just as I am

in my department, the problem is not much
better in New York City, during meetings

of the 2019 Whitman Consortium consisting
of 70+ organizations planning to celebrate

the bicentennial of Whitman's birth, I was
the only POC at the table, a couple others sat

on the margins but they were not the heads
of their organizations, only I, Asian American,

got to sit in the circle with all the esteemed
White heads representing some of the most

prestigious literary wealth in the country,
we shared how we were going to celebrate

the "Poet of Democracy," the "one White father"
in June Jordan's estimation who shared

the "systematic disadvantages of his heterogeneous
offspring trapped inside a closet," and all I

could think was *This is us 200 years later?*
What would Jordan have thought of this room?

There were plenty of women in charge, but all
White. A few gay men I knew, White. And me.

And I had to create my own organization
and build it big enough to gain White approval

to get a seat at that table. I didn't feel proud
of this, or like I had any power, but small,

smaller than I usually do when I'm dreaming
big dreams alone or among my peoples

because I'm not seeing the stakes of the game
laid out with such physical reproof, there

was no moving any weight at that table,
someone asked if the Consortium was going

to say anything about Whitman's problematic
views on race and another person said yes

thank you for bringing up that issue and
another said I think it would be best to get out

in front of this, as if it were a PR problem,
I put in my one cent about the importance

of getting people of color involved, especially
young ones, connecting Whitman to those

"heterogeneous offspring" Jordan imagined
he stood for, but I didn't say it in just this way,

I didn't mention Jordan's quote, I didn't want
to come off as confrontational, in fact I don't

remember exactly what I said, it might as well
have been silence for all the difference it made,

I've taken part in event after event celebrating
Whitman over the past few months and save

for the one I myself organized, there were no
or almost no POC speaking or performing

other than me, and perhaps more alarmingly,
almost no POC present in the audiences,

and these events were in New York City, not
Hamden, I went to speak in support of a coalition

trying to get Whitman's last standing NYC home
at 99 Ryerson St. considered for landmarking

at a Landmarks Preservation Commission hearing
on six proposed LGBTQ sites (not including

Whitman's), and I was the only POC offering
public testimony in our group, I did that

obligatory room check and saw just one
older Asian gentleman and one Black woman

at the otherwise White table of commissioners,
another Black woman sitting off to the side

of the table who presented research on why
Audre Lorde's last home in Staten Island

should be landmarked, and one Black man
wearing a Vietnam Veterans cap sitting

with the rest of us in the public, he rose
to speak on the Lorde case, we'd already heard

several prepared statements of support
delivered by smart White folks representing

LGBTQ interests but I was most interested
in what this man had to say as the lone Black

man in the audience, I assumed he was
going to offer support but then got a lesson

in the complexities of identity politics
that Lorde spent a lifetime trying to work

out, he didn't *not* offer support, he said
he wasn't against landmarking the house

but he *was* against the LPC writing him,
the owner of that house for over twenty years,

to say he'd built an illegal deck at the back
of it, the house was already designated

as "historic" by the LPC in 2004 as part
of the St. Paul's Avenue–Stapleton Heights

Historic District and thus already protected
from major alterations, hence this letter,

you might wonder why the house had to be
landmarked if it was already protected

and I assume this was to give it some kind
of additional protection, honor its cultural,

not just architectural, significance, and also
to mark it as a political "win" for the LGBTQ

community in the year celebrating the 50th
anniversary of the Stonewall Uprising,

but this man didn't care about any of that,
he didn't mention Lorde once or show pride

in what the house represented, he took pride
in that deck, how much money and time

and care he'd invested in it, he said if you'd
looked at the back of the house (not pictured

in the slideshow) when he'd bought it, you'd
have seen a window that looked like it was

originally a door, probably leading to a deck
that had been removed, all the other houses

on his historic block had decks except his,
so in his mind he'd been doing the work

of restoration, not alteration, he was the one
who'd painted the house the way it looks

today, who'd kept it so convincingly "historic,"
he didn't know why he was being penalized

and he was worried landmarking the house
would make it even more difficult for him

to save his deck, he got the loudest applause
of any speaker in the room but I wondered

what the LGBTQ contingent thought of him,
whether they felt sympathy or perceived him

as a threat, Lorde herself would've been
keenly aware of all the ironies in play, White

LGBTQ activists like those she often clashed
with over race working to honor her role

in their cause and race again irritatingly
getting in the way in the form of a Black man

troubling their unified front, protecting
his own interests and exposing the Whiteness

of their own, a man she may have clashed with
too, who didn't seem to know or care at all

who she was, who might've seen her sexuality
as a betrayal of their own unified Black front

against White interests, I don't know who
Lorde would've sided with or if they were even

opposed but I doubt she would've been for
having her home landmarked if it meant

this Black Vietnam vet would have to suffer
the loss of his deck, I think she would've been

suspicious of any coalition of White interests
advancing upon a Black citizen's autonomy,

and she definitely would've said something,
she would've braved the return fire, though

I don't know if she would've said anything
about this bar, if she would've thought it worth

the unrest, but maybe calculations like this
prove our difference, my greater alignment

with Whiteness, my ability to choose rest
or unrest, when for her, the rest was silence.

from *Copper Nickel*

Skeletons

◇   ◇   ◇

So whatever's the opposite of a Buddhist that's what I am.
Kindhearted, yes, but knee deep in existential gloom,
except when the fog smokes the bridges like this—
like, instead of being afraid we might juice ourselves up,
eh, like, might get kissed again? Dwelling in bones I go straight
through life, a kind of sublime abundance—cherries, dog's breath, the sun, then
(ouch) & all of us snuffed out. Dear one, what is waiting for us tonight,
nostalgia? the homes of childhood? oblivion? How we hate to go—

★

Sundays I spend feeling sorry for myself I've got a
knack for it I'm morbid, make the worst of any season
exclamation point   yet levity's a liquor of sorts,
lowers us through life toward the terminus soon
extinguished   darling, the comfort is slight,
tucked in bed we search each other for some alternative—
oh let's marvel at the world, the stroke and colors of it
now, while breathing.

from *The New Yorker*

Big Clock

◇ ◇ ◇

When the big clock at the train station stopped,
the leaves kept falling,
the trains kept running,
my mother's hair kept growing longer and blacker,
and my father's body kept filling up with time.

I can't see the year on the station's calendar.
We slept under the stopped hands of the clock
until morning, when a man entered carrying a ladder.
He climbed up to the clock's face and opened it with a key.
No one but he knew what he saw.

Below him, the mortal faces went on passing
toward all compass points.
People went on crossing borders,
buying tickets in one time zone and setting foot in another.
Crossing thresholds: sleep to waking and back,
waiting room to moving train and back,
war zone to safe zone and back.

Crossing between gain and loss:
learning new words for the world and the things in it.
Forgetting old words for the heart and the things in it.
And collecting words in a different language
for those three primary colors:
staying, leaving, and returning.

And only the man at the top of the ladder
understood what he saw behind the face
which was neither smiling nor frowning.

And my father's body went on filling up with death
until it reached the highest etched mark
of his eyes and spilled into mine.
And my mother's hair goes on
never reaching the earth.

from Poem-a-Day

DANA LEVIN

January Garden

◇ ◇ ◇

Woke up with: *the minute I let "I love you" touch me, trees*
                          sprouted from my hair—

Woke up with: *Zeus fatigue—*   (what ails the nation)

Woke up with: *the soul a balm, a lozenge, yet another*
                          pill-shaped thing—

Woke up and   recalled nothing—   took a walk in winter air—

                    in the January garden. No one
                       on benches—

                    And then remembered—with a bolt—how I'd been
                       titling a poem in my sleep:

                         A Little Less, Day After Day, Bomb After Bomb

                    And just as I remembered, I passed a young woman
                       at a picnic table, writing in a journal—

                    And she held—so help me!—a pen shaped
                       like a bone—

                    And I heard the poem:

                         Each of us, by nature, a killer—

Each of us, by nature,
picking something to practice

mercy on—

from *Air/Light*

My Father's Mustache

◇ ◇ ◇

Let us pause to applaud the white bell-bottom suit,
the wide flared collar, the black thick-coiffed hair
in this photo my father has sent of himself
at a gathering off Sonoma Highway in the early '70s.
I can't stop looking at the photo. There is a swagger
that feels almost otherworldly, epic, like Lorca
expounding in Buenos Aires, *not form*
but the marrow of form. He is perfect there, my father
in the photo. I feel somehow as if I'm perched on a bay laurel
branch nearby though not born yet. It's in black and white, the photo.
You can see his grin behind his lush mustache. Is it time
that moves in me now? A sense of ache and unraveling,
my father in his pristine white suit, the eye of the world barely able
to handle his smooth unbroken stride. It's been a year
since I've seen him in person, I miss how he points
to his apple trees and I miss his smooth face
that no longer has the mustache I always adored.
As a child I once cried when he shaved it. Even then,
I was too attached to this life.

from *The New Republic*

the junkyard galaxy knocks

◊　◊　◊

for a long hour my dog sits, head cocked
as a ready hand, stares toward the plum-
drenched window where nothing is visible

to me but a neighbor's TV pulse of blue
light. I wonder what he sees beyond—
or in—the pane. when I first rented

this place with its sweeping ceiling of
exposed beams, I asked the landlady
who'd lived here before, last century,

and it was blind men & women workers
for a local factory. then again, you don't know
what you can't see. my dog blinks at the dark,

swivels ears toward the black hole of glass.
sometimes the ceiling drops nubs of carbonized
wood like asteroids onto my white sofa. I pluck

them off carefully. I have a bouquet of
comet shards flung from my roof, but who
brings space debris indoors? I start to believe

it's whoever's in the window, and yes,
there are times the other windows howl
a loose-jointed chorus of clattering thwacks,

sounding both fragile and like a fist
punching the glass. I tell my lover over
the wind, *if I ever wake up as a dog*

you'll know it's me. keep the dog with you
if I do. and how will he see that it's me,
he wants to know. I say,

just look.   a window is a portal—
somewhere in space-time there are animals who
see what we can't conjure even in sleep.

who decides where a roof ends
and the junkyard galaxy begins—
when I say *hello love* and he peers under

the blinds of my eyelashes, is what he sees
what I think he sees? when I say *ability*
sometimes I mean a spot in the spherical,

gaseous planet of ability. I blink into
myself, trying to unsmudge the fenestra.
who's there? I ask my dog. *who's there?*

from *Blackbird*

How to Greet a Warbler

◇　◇　◇

for Christian Cooper

Today, walking in the tall grass
close to home, mask on, ears wide
I spotted a warbler all yellow-bellied
with its human eyes & soft-tongued
song & I imagined how we could have
lost another one of us to the kind of
violence only whiteness is allowed
to dream up & enact. His wings were

rousing up dirt in protest as if he too
was envisioning loss & I swear I wanted
to kneel before him & make of him
　　　　　　　　a church—

from *Colorado Review*

Myths About Trees

◇   ◇   ◇

I would walk across refrigerator water with you
To the other side. I would build a blue kitchen
And flower in it, a single bud. I would burst—
Have our colt over again so you could hum
To it. I would love you only just enough through
The steep Iowa winter. You would barely notice
How cold we were getting. I would cut down the wood to
Find your ship. But there are no trees left in my childhood;
I tore them down looking for my brother when asking
Got me nowhere. And I loved trees. They were all I
Could write about. The only place my thrush would sleep.
I would want to find out we were having a boy, gently this time,
And I would bring you peace.
I don't know if I can do this again, with anyone. It isn't fair
To show them how I was brought here, against my will.
Our son has your eyes, my mouth. Out of my mouth
He says he sees you. I was sure he would look at us
And see who hurt who. That used to be a door.
No, I do not understand when you speak to me. I do not
Know the easy way through this landscape. I don't know why
I live here. And I have lived here so long, most of my time.
You are a ghost. I do not know how we ever made love,
Or if we did.

from *West Branch*

Trauma Note

◊ ◊ ◊

You ask if the author really wants to cup the moon. We both know it's not true, but it's so nice to give the reader a beautiful lie. I am a great beauty eating a heart of solid fire with my pretty serrated knife. See, the heart sometimes lies so good that giant trails of fire burn through neighborhoods. Following an ancient path. It can be the total yearning for someone to hold up a lifted sheet. It can be sold in a bundle. Or, the smell of burnt toast. It cannot be being. It sounds like smoke because we invent detectors. Fire makes a bad lover the rumor goes. Deny everything is the utility company's policy. Not a lie: We fled for gas stations under the fire's yellow night light. Cars lined up forever down River Road. Landlords rent gouge. What can you do? One guy saved a pack of antelope by pushing the male leader through a firewall until the others followed. He owns a safari park in wine country. It's true. You can go there. It was not dark. He had plenty of firelight to see. Another couple waded in their pool for hours. No moon. Just two heads bobbing above chlorinated water, two heads fenced by flames. There's a one hundred year flood coming soon, a flood we don't know about yet. Do you know why I like it here? No, not the knives. It's a haunted color here, and I like haunted colors.

from *Maiden Magazine*

Quoting the Bible

◊　◊　◊

Tonight I'm thinking about Jesus
which isn't remarkable
for most people on Christmas
but it is for me.
Which means that I'm really
thinking about the light
from Seamus Heaney's phone
when he texted his wife
don't be afraid seconds before
he left his body behind.
Don't be afraid,
I tell my son
as I buckle his seatbelt,
don't be afraid
I place a green dinosaur
mask on his face,
don't be afraid, I spray
his hands with disinfectant
don't be afraid
I hold him close
and walk away from
other mothers singing
their own version of
don't be afraid
I say it so often
I wonder if my son
thinks the words
are a series

of sounds I hum
when I'm around him
to get through the day
more comfort
than language, more
shape than mouth,
more memory than body,
more mother than person.

from *The Threepenny Review*

ROBIN MYERS

Diego de Montemayor

◇   ◇   ◇

ca. 1530–1611

If a man is capable of massacre
    or overseeing
        massacre, which is
the same, does this also make
        him capable
of killing his own wife?
Put another way,
    if a man can seize
        a sword and stab his wife to
death on learning she'd taken
        a lover during one of his imperial
incursions into the sierra, massacring or
overseeing massacre,
    which is the same, disseminating
        smallpox, brandishing
Catholicism, lashing the speakers
        of languages spoken in the lands
he'd resolved to possess
in the name of the Spanish crown,
    well, fuck
        the hypotheticals, because
he did it, all
    of it, and it's his name
    I know, not his wife's or anyone else's
he massacred or raped
    or ordered massacred or raped or
        the children they

birthed or their children who
          continued to birth, over time, so
many children that they were
branded a nation
          and flung into diaspora and dust-settled down
                    into generations of children
          of which I'm one,
                    because that's
          how
family
          works.

from *The Yale Review*

Best Friend Ballad

◊   ◊   ◊

Sometimes I'll suddenly remember the power
of her house, and of the approach to it,
down the narrow, extreme-curve-to-the-
right street, opening onto the

somehow delicate cul-de-sac, my
best friend's
house—what?
Italianate? Ogive windows,

balconies, tile roof,
the land fallen off steep behind it to the
gradual slope to the Bay. And then
the flat stones up to her Doric

portico—between them flowering
weeds, no ice plant, no ivy, just tiny
blossoms, then there it was, like a villa,
a little Berkeley palace, a doctor's

elegant home of safety where she was
dying, 9 years old, and I didn't
let myself realize it.
If her mother had been there, maybe I could have

asked her if I could take a nap
with my friend when she fell

asleep—but her mother
had died the day before, my job

was to not let my friend know it—

so she could die as if she had
a mother. And what would I have given
to have been allowed to lie down
next to her dear skeletal body.

She still had her fine, chartreuse,
thick, almost sour-color hair,
as if the lead poison they'd breathed had
sharpened the chartreuse of it—

what would I have given to be
allowed to fall asleep with her
and dream, alive—what would I give
now? Nothing, I have nothing to give,

none of the luck which followed in my fortunate
life. But I pray for a sleep tonight in which,
9 and 9, we can hold each other in a
green dream.

from *The Threepenny Review*

In Virginia

◇ ◇ ◇

In Virginia's room

Her own

Peruvian lilies light her desk

With carefully placed pens

Bought with her own words

The groovings in the desk waxed by

Pearline who at noon serves Earl Grey

In a pink apron carrying pink teacups

Laced with lemon on its pungent lip

Delicate woman-sized treats for swooning

Pearline moves to the door to bring in the silk road porcelain tub

Camphor, salts and tints-of-violet to balm Virginia's tuckered feet

Unbend the curvature of Virginia's back the enamored covetous prose

In Virginia's own

Pearlie she calls bring my notebooks and more tea

Pearline walks hard into the kitchen to draw the fires prepare domesticity

For the writer who needs a room of her own to subordinate her muse

Her maid who labors for Miss Virginia's ownness, her roominess

Virginia says the room frees her from the tyranny of man

Her men, planters and industrialists

Pearline is asked to stay late to prepare refreshments for her writer friends

To collect their wet coats and dry them by the hearth

And pleasantly waitress their personalities

Pearline agreeable prepares the table embosses it with fairies

and musing mermaids tapered flickering

Nights when Pearline walks to her bus stop fresh from clanking silver goblets of drink

She has never tasted goes to the butcher for the leftover shanks of meat closest to

The guts of its porcine body for her own family's stewed victuals

At home she draws the fire for her children's nightly bath

Washes clothes for school on the morrow, braids their hair

After all and sundry has been cared for she walks to the pallet she shares

And thinks of Virginia's ownness the ownness that she

Pearline keeps pristine from the tyranny of mistress Virginia's men

from *The Rumpus*

Pandemic Parable

◇　◇　◇

I'll check on the flowers, the mother says to no one as she leaves the house.

Out the back gate, she skulks through alleys instead of streets.

By flowers she doesn't mean mistflower bounced over by monarchs, not calico lantana.

Not indigo dayflower, not the particulate white hedge parsley in the alley bracken.

One morning, the mother's daughters owned a roly-poly.

Pill bug, doodle bug, wood shrimp: going by many names seems a freedom.

When she believed she was free to choose the kind of mother she would be, the mother
　　chose a name from a list: Mama, Mommy, Ma, Mom, Mum, Mummy, etc.

Her daughters made a house using the biggest American beautyberry leaf they'd ever seen,
　　an asphalt chunk, and a petal from the neighbor's knockout rose.

Is your roly-poly still living there? is a question she knows better than to ask her daughters.

Her daughters are still so young that they've cried almost every day they've been alive.

Conglobation is the name for curling up into a tiny blue-black ball in a child's palm.

The mother cries herself that spring, though crying doesn't make her feel like a girl.

Jane Eyre: "It is not without a certain wild pleasure that I run before the wind."

Whither pleasure? is a question the mother knows better than to ask herself that spring.

A child never thinks, I'm supposed to do X but I want to do Y.

Licking the knife, forgoing sunscreen, throwing out her daughters' rumpled drawings: the mother's pleasures feel most wrong when executed in secret.

A child rips the silky pink petals off the neighbor's knockout rose.

The scent confederate jasmine overtakes the air.

Confederate is the name for someone or something united in a league, alliance, or confederacy.

The name makes her wary of the flowers.

Hers is a country with an unshakeable history.

We've been waiting for you, say the flowers to no one.

Like the datura, lantana, and morning glory, the confederate jasmine is toxic if eaten.

To what extent has she already been poisoned?

Out creeps the evergreen want: to disappear for a bit, not come when called.

Mr. Rolls is what they called the roly-poly when they wanted it to come to them.

To explain the pleasure the mother took in disappearing from her home required her to explain the danger she felt when it was the only thing she wanted.

It rolled in a ball and did not come.

Her daughters collected the bright red seeds of the Texas mountain laurel and left them all over the house.

They knew the seeds were poisonous but didn't know their names.

People were dying that spring but they didn't know their names.

If she ran away from home, how would the mother teach them not to run away?

Maybe the mother was wrong.

Jostling paints and glitter, her daughters upset the face painter at a long-ago birthday party.

Holding a delicate brush, the painter looked at one daughter and sighed, *What do you want on your face?*

Her daughter said, *My face.*

from *Mississippi Review*

Elegy on Fire

◇ ◇ ◇

I escaped from a building on fire
with only my jeans pulled on and
not even shoes on my feet
as I stood there, thinking of that
Peggy Lee song Is That All There
Is a stranger put a blanket on me
I wasn't on fire and didn't need
to be put out but it was clear I
needed comfort of some sort and
a human in the vicinity gave it

This is a Fourth of July tale the
hazards of smoldering ordnance in
the dumpster next to the kitchen
window the careless casual way
we toss live ammo in the air and
golly gee ain't that a shimmerer
ain't that a beaut my father would
say who grew up in the land of
fireworks and taught me before I
could walk and talk the way to
light a fuse is hold it with your
fingernails so if it burns fast it
might burn you but it won't ex
plode and always immerse the
shells in water after just in case

He who loved bombs went to Nam
collected guns I always thought
like poets come out with collected
poems my father should come out
with collected guns but now he's
buried in Sai Pan though I think
he'd appreciate the way my humor
bombs sometimes a weeping willow
he said looking up at the sky while
the bombs were bursting in air

What would he make of this display
of affection years after we ran out of
things to say and what would he
make of this country he served and
questioned at the same time the way
we love and don't love our parents
who are after all just grown kids a
little smarter than us perhaps but not
by much especially when they vote

I want to wake up the neighbors
the way they once woke me the
building's on fire get out get out
I want to have already rebuilt after
patriotism has hurled its sparklers
in the trash and scorched us all

On my way home on base I'd hear
retreat on the public address and
stand at attention as it played out
over the quonset huts and fences
over the bombers that sat on alert
and the supersonic reconnaissance
craft and the boys playing stickball
unexploded ordnance left over from
a previous war the tripwires cross
the fields like spider silk but finer

I put my hand over my heart I put
my heart over my head I loved in
the midst of war the war's music
the Iliad lay on my bunk open to
the body of Hector on his shield

I was a boy it was an island it was
far from home but it was quarters
and soldiers beaches of white sand
and boy the fireworks they broke
into a thousand threads cascading
over the fields of Troy but then I
woke in a city on fire and when I
went to carry my father out he was
already on a pyre he lit himself
it's a wonder the rest of us got out

from *The Adroit Journal*

After Graduate School

◇　◇　◇

Needless to say I support the forsythia's war
against the dull colored houses, the beagle
deciphering the infinitely complicated universe
at the bottom of a fence post. I should be gussying up
my resume, I should be dusting off my protestant work ethic,
not walking around the neighborhood loving the peonies
and the lilac bushes, not heading up Shamrock
and spotting Lucia coming down the train tracks. Lucia
who just sold her first story and whose rent is going up,
too, Lucia who says she's moving to South America to save money,
Lucia, cute twenty-something I wish wasn't walking down train tracks
alone. I tell her about my niece teaching in China, about the waiter
who built a tiny house in Hawaii, how he saved up, how
he had to call the house a garage to get a building permit.
Someone's practicing the trumpet, someone's frying bacon
and once again the wisteria across the street is trying to take over
the nation. Which could use a nice invasion, old growth trees
and sea turtles, every kind of bird marching
on Washington. If I had something in my refrigerator,
if my house didn't look like the woman who lives there
forgot to water the plants, I'd invite Lucia home,
enjoy another hour of not thinking about not having a job,
about not having a mother to move back in with.
I could pick Lucia's brain about our circadian rhythms,
about this space between sunrise and sunset,
ask if she's ever managed to get inside it, the air,
the sky ethereal as all get out—*so close*
and no ladder in sight.

from Poem-a-Day

The Remaining Facts

◇ ◇ ◇

On the hour, the full, shuffled week since you said goodbye, I said goodbye. A pillow in your lap &, six days later, the boarding pass in the pocket of your black sweatshirt. I remember touching your leg to wake you &, if we erase the walls, you faced the ocean at the edge of the bed waiting for your clothes. The torn nail from days ago (now nearly healed) & my difficulty hooking your bra. Three, four steps outside & I've been driving slower, like you asked, & letting go. Senseless coincidence here in its rightful place & little more, not figurative nor overblown yet we were waiting on one of many storms. Later, we left the highway for a wooded drive & I learned the difference between widow & widower. Then I kissed your head through a paper mask.

from *The Tiny*

Follow Them

◇　◇　◇

over a football game, Autumn
evening, of this kind of thing I'm not ashamed
nor of the twistiness of that diction,
or wanting America to burn
though only certain parts deserve to die,
its forests are beautiful and have done
nothing wrong, even the desert's emptiness
is beautiful, though it terrifies me,
and tacos, and kebabs wrapped up in naan,
and today walking through the park I turned
to see dozens of bright white seagulls flocked
on the windy lake against the blue sky
and I felt an ache and I sent a text
to a friend I said TODAY I SAW FLOCKED
ON THE LAKE WHITE SEAGULLS IT WAS BEAUTIFUL
he wrote FOLLOW THEM it was too late

from The American Poetry Review

La Época En Que Hay Olvida

◊　◊　◊

Sometimes I enter the small chambers of the God of Forgetting
and take my place at his feet
and kneel
and bow my head.

And I say into the ground that bears both of us:
I need you—now. You

who have listened to the supplications
of tyrants, dictators
and kings—in my lifetime alone,
granted countless wishes.

But there is already a country renamed for its suffering,
and an altar upon which
the innocent secretly
undo the knots
with their teeth.

All I have to offer are rotting carrots
and a basil plant
dying in stale water.

I used to eavesdrop on the priests who moonlight as assassins
to make sure my name
doesn't appear in their diaries.

How many people have come outside
from their desperate invocations
and self-mutilation

to see the wonder for themselves? Is it true?
Are the juncos
singing
in the dogwoods?

Have the dancers removed their right shoes?
Are they hopping around
on both hands?

Yes, it *is* true. We are closing our eyes. To forecast death
we gather with strangers,
like this one woman
in the mustard coat
sitting on a park bench.

Her son has opened a small blue box stuffed with peanuts
and he pours them into her one cupped hand
so a few fall
for the sparrows
and all the while

the chainsaw is singing to each of us: STAY! STAY AS LONG AS YOU LIKE!
NO ONE CAN KEEP YOU!
and the boy—I told you—
is trying to fly.

He first lifts one wing, then lets both go. Now
watch the little one
take off

leading his enormous dragon made of water and light
by its silver leash. See

the long liquid flock of glistening muscle
ripples from the child's fist.

from *Virginia Quarterly Review*

Departure

◇   ◇   ◇

Oh, my needy pocket, the crooked
tunnel that is not, in fact,
a tunnel. You have brought me
joy. You have brought me.
Who am I to question? First—
Chill—Then Stupor—Then
the evacuation. And
a man with a stained shirt.
My legs spread. Are you sure?
he asked. Yes, I said.
Will she come back? Will she
come back? Will she come
back? Will she come back? Will
she come back? Will she
come back? Will she come
back? Will she come back?
Will she come back? Will she
come back? Will she come back?
Will she come back? Will she—
I heard it all—the jar of me.
I put on my pants and gave
thanks. I held my grief like
two limp tulips. What am I
allowed to have? I'm still
here. I'm still hers. I'm
still a body licked by stars.

My eyes always drawn
to the groveling. Bless
these burnt wings. Bless.
Would I do it again?
Yes. Yes. Yes.

from Poem-a-Day

Hair Sestina

◇ ◇ ◇

I'm twenty-four and yes, by now I know
I have a problem. "Oh, but don't we all?"
everyone jokes as if it's really brilliant.
But not like this. A slippery chunk of life
has slid on by, and still I am without
an inkling of real knowledge about black

hairstyles. Some bus driver says, "You're 'black'
in name, but you will never *really* know
their struggles." *Their*. It sticks. I'm left without
a comeback (since I know it's true). She's all
proud now and continues on, "Your life
seems easier than most." Gee, *that* is brilliant.

I'm not sure if I'm hurt or not. A brilliant
professor told me once (her hair dyed black
as licorice bites), "Sometimes, you know, in life,
you'll want to cry but can't. Just so you know,
the answer is to bite your thumb. That's all."
My cluelessness, though? Soon, I'll be without

a thumb, a life, a man to dine with. (Out
of time.) I only care about hair now. Brilliant
black scholar is what I aim for. I spend all
my leisure time these days researching *black
hair looks*. I nod, I practice, hope I'll know
a twist-out when I see it. I watch *Life*

(the one with Eddie Murphy), plan a life
where someday I'll have cornrows, braids, without
the insecurity. Should I—oh no,
no flashcards. What's the point of being brilliant
when I wear white girl hair to Sam's Club, lack
inheritance and understanding? All

I know is this: it wouldn't be right to call
what happened to me *abandonment*. See, life
can be too hard for us, including my black
father, once-Marine, six two, without
someone to speak to, even me. Not brilliant,
but he could have helped me come to know

my hair, my blackness, self. Oh, well. Without
some emptiness, what's life? Twenty-four. "Brilliant."
"Accomplished." All I know is what I don't.

from *Northwest Review*

Modern Poetry

◊ ◊ ◊

It was what I'd been waiting for my whole life,
but I wasn't ready for poetry. I didn't have
the tools. Roethke,
I appreciated the greenhouse poems,

and decades later saw his bed, toilet, upright
piano in that desolate town where he was raised,
not unlike the desolate town where I was raised.
No greenhouse in my town, but the Green Giant

factory, where mushrooms grew on cow shit.
Wallace Stevens, I wrote a paper on "Loneliness
in Jersey City" having no clue
what he meant by "the deer and the dachshund are one"

and got an A anyway by faking it.
The professor made us read
"Sunday Morning," which struck me
as long. I couldn't focus yet, I was eighteen. A poem

against heaven, he told us. "Is there no change of death
in paradise? Does ripe fruit never fall?" That I could
understand, having known some plums,
and that icky-sweet smell of a dead mouse in the wall.

Gerard Manley Hopkins, not modern per se
but my professor said, one of the first modernists,
so what did modern poetry really mean, maybe
just fucked up, as Hopkins was for sure, and tongue

twistery, and depressed, Jesuit, maybe bipolar.
I stared at his photograph, the long nose and cleft
in his chin, noticed that even in "No worst, there is none"
he had the wherewithal to put in the accent marks

to school us as to how to hear the thing. And WCW.
Williams. My roommate and I called him Billy C. Billygoat.
I knew something of wheelbarrows, old women,
and as I said, plums, but the prof showed us

how complicated it all really was, the whole "no ideas
but in things" thing, the near-rhymes,
depends and *chickens* and *red*, again, I was not yet
capable of being smart and wondered if I ever would be,

though I kept getting A's on the papers, maybe
because the professor felt sorry for me, and I'm not just
saying that. The final modern poet was Sylvia Plath,
a woman, blonde, and I didn't trust blondes,

smart, angry, angry at men, I was told, depressed, cheated
on, dead. I imagined her being in Modern Poetry with us,
mopping the floor with us, with her developed
mind, her ooh and ahh sounds, her thesis, "The Magic Mirror,"

on the double in Dostoevsky. I pictured her calling me
a charlatan, like Gaylord did in class the week we studied her.
He called her a charlatan psychopath, and me a charlatan
for sticking up for her. I had to go back

to the dorm and look up "charlatan" in the dictionary.
A fraud, the dictionary said. A quack, which yes, I was,
though so was Gaylord. Who isn't a quack at eighteen?
I wanted to love Sylvia, but to love her would mean

loving someone who would have hated me.
It would be a few years, after I flunked out
of college, until I took a class called Women's Literature
at the public university down the hill with a teacher

named Stephanie who looked a lot like Françoise Sagan,
teenage author of *Bonjour Tristesse*, but older and with a cap
of gray hair. Margaret Atwood. Toni Morrison. Adrienne Rich.
Charlotte Perkins Gilman. Plath. Sexton. Lorde.

Kate Chopin. Alice Walker. Djuna Barnes. I was beginning
to understand, but barely. To ask a pertinent question
now and then, like where the hell was Langston Hughes
in Modern Poetry? Dickinson, in 19th Century American Lit?

If Hopkins was a Modernist, how about Dickinson,
with her weird rhymes and what Galway Kinnell called
her "inner, speech-like, sliding, syncopated rhythm,"
a counterpoint to her iambic lines? A horse straining at the bit

in the direction of free verse. A woman who drove
a motorcycle to Women's Literature, wore a fringed
black leather jacket, and worked at the Kalamazoo airport
in the cubicle where people pay for parking was shot and killed there

by her ex-boyfriend. From then on the class became
something else. Stephanie had us over to her house,
a damp place in the woods. She roasted a goat
and served it to us, shredded, on blue plates.

The books had become more, and less, important.
We spoke of them, huddled on the floor by the fire.
I remember most of all the bushel baskets
of apples and grapes for winemaking, drawing fruit flies.

I'm not complaining. It was all more than I deserved.
The goat. The greenhouse. The liberated blonde badass
on her motorcycle. *Sula. Surfacing.* Sunday Morning.
Ripe plums. My education.

from *The Adirondack Review*

Widowing

◇　◇　◇

My inner controversy of packing up
the last of your studio boxes
towering this new basement that I clean for good. All this in
  year four.

In them I find a lone condom,
a buried treasure of your lost virility.

Was it saying something lonely to me?
And then not to me but to a stranger, another one?

When you were alive
I had found a condom in your computer bag.
You balked— in your stupid rage—
and told me it was so old—from when we used them, back in 2002.

I knew they only have a span of five years; they swim upstream in
  their packages.

This one expired in 2016. You died in 2015. When did you buy
  this last condom?

(Nobody talks about the difficult grieving process of mourning
  your husband and then his secrets and vices, left in corner
  plastic bins.)

But this is why I built a synthetic cave around my
  disappointments

like the chemicals that drowned your sense and reason
and left only an outward charm of deflection like a collected
    banality.

Your sister, a nurse, after washing your body,
cleaned up your Fentanyl patches with their glassine
coverings on the laundry room floor, behind the washer and dryer.

You took it with your chemotherapy, but you were also sneaking
    it for years.

You were always searching for painkillers, hiding them high up
    from me.

Or in your bins, at your studio, full of drawings, cartoons, and
    scribbled poems

that make so obvious how you lived inside yourself with a kind
    of agony,

in your own fallible body, its chronic pain, and what it really
    called forth,
an insatiable carrying of a private penury, your only sojourn.

from *The Yale Review*

In the Lockdown

◇ ◇ ◇

I might've gone stir crazy,
If not for Solitude,
That grand dame
Long accustomed to her fate

And eager to console me
Down in the dumps
With stories of men and women
Throughout the ages

Who withdrew from the world
And endured years of seclusion
And dark nights of the soul
Before they found inner peace

In some hole in the wall
Mulling over someone's advice:
"Go sit quietly and your room
Will teach you everything."

from *Salmagundi*

Anthropocene: A Dictionary

◊   ◊   ◊

dibé bighan: sheep corral

juniper beams caught charcoal in the late summer morning
night still pooled in hoof prints; deer panicked run from water

ooljéé' biná'adinídíín: moonlight

perched above the town drowned in orange and streetlamp
       the road back home dips with the earth
          shines black in the sirens

bit'a' : its sails or—its wing (s)

      driving through the mountain pass
         dólii, mountain bluebird, swings out—
      from swollen branches
I never see those anymore, someone says

diyóół   :   wind (

wind (more of it) more wind as in (to come up)
plastic bags driftwood the fence line

nihootsoii

        :   evening—somewhere northward fire
                        twists around the shrublands;
                  sky dipped in smoke—twilight

                        —there is a word for this,
                                someone says

:   deidíílid, *they burned it*
:   kódeiilyaa, *we did this*

from Poem-a-Day

Hungry Poem with Laughter Coming from an Unknown Source

◊   ◊   ◊

She's still there the further you look back. I mean before the war,

and the wolves, and the other war, and the French, and her departure,

and even the Chinese—I mean *that* way back. And since I'm talking

about my mother, let's talk a hair-down, cat-eyed perfection, heels on a

borrowed Vespa kind of laughter—filling whole highways

with her eyeliner (another kind of laughter) and a deep belly

laugh at the thought of the Trưng Sisters ever jumping from

a single thing besides the time it takes my mother to flip the switch

on a boring conversation with a dick joke—*what did she say?*—

I mean keep up, I mean *that* far back—when Vietnam knew a world

could be best run by women and more women with still more laughter

charging the void—a still-life silt, a nitty-knot of a lump in the throat—

that sensation between choking and uncontrollable, heaving laughter at the very thing that controls you and your body and your mother's body and

my sisters—my dear sisters—we always had laughter for our bodies that kept

planting deeper into the woods // *groundcover* // insert cut-scene, rescind the fairy

tale: we all know there are no true villains—we're just a bunch of hungry animals.

I would jump with you, I would. I would give it all for you—laughter at

sundown, laughter at the feet crushing statuary, laughter until our very

last word on this dying Earth that just keeps turning and turning its

silhouette shadow figures slipping back into human skin at dawn.

from *Hobart After Dark*

Little Time

◇ ◇ ◇

We must go for a walk
in the freshly washed
world, he says.

We must venture into
the thicket with cacti
in our open corneas.

There is so much to see,
little time.

Little time, trickling from an eave.
Little time, dropping from leaves,
falling, collecting, becoming
serious puddles for
paper boats to cross.

We must build a paper boat
in the freshly puddled
world, he says.

We must write our secret
names on the hull.

Little boat, braving the wavescapes.
Little time, before water softens paper.

Was it earlier, a newsman reported
a young mother's body washed
to shore during the storms.

I imagined her shoes,
little boats.

The newsman spoke to us.
        He said: *And now, way ahead*
of time, she was gone.

from *Pleiades*

Lest I Forget Thee

◇　◇　◇

Ignoring the still waters
and the kingdom of Babylon
some call America
I practice my different strokes
in the three river systems of Pennsylvania
and once in a wool bathing suit
at the far end of the Steel Pier
a city block away from the safe sand
and my two uncles buried there
except for their noses.

Still waters also
in the quarry off route 32
where our cars and bikes
lined up in the dirt
beside the concrete,
but there was no Babylon,
no one there mourning for their village,
only naked bodies leaping from rocks
and either hugging the shore
or swimming madly the half-mile or so
into the tall grasses
on the other side,
me among them.
And since there was very little music
we gathered around one of the tapes
sharing the sound until we dove back in,

but I no longer heard it
as I approached the grasses
though I heard something else.

from *The American Poetry Review*

The Infant's Eyes

◇   ◇   ◇

Now that I too am
the terrible witness
to the ovum
and I have been
wrestled to the ground
with her fresh bread
and dirt
breath and have been
the laughing maniac
of motherhood
now
I will always
rise and go
to see what is wrong
like a cardinal to the pope
whenever something sounds
from upstairs
I'll rush up
or out
or in
to see what is what
whether anyone is hurt
or in need
then I will putter back
to continue the leftover
saggy and unreal job
of aging
toward benediction.

Now
when I bite into
the tied-off end
of a sausage
it reminds me
of her umbilical cord.
As the eyes
of the mice
in my kitchen
remind me of her eyes
in the unclearness
of the birthing room—
when the mice watch me
storm about, slamming
dishes, it reminds me
how her infant eyes
began
to follow me
when I paced
the little
horrible apartment
we were living in
when she was born
an apartment
that reeked in the hallway
of cigarettes
and the neighbor was always
screaming at her boyfriend
that he was
"making her fat"
because he didn't
love her enough
and he would hang
out his window
smoking a bowl
saying "Geezus
fuckinChrist"
and shaking
his head

those were the days
when my baby began
following me with her eyes
when I—neurotic
about her breathing—noticed her
noticing me—
and realized I'd never been
looked at like that before.
As if the sky
had ripped off
a strip of its blue
and a massive face
looked through at me—
I froze under her
dispassionate
infant stare

her twin black crystal balls
focusing fully on me
surveying like
an ancient god
the status
of evolution's
latest results,
making what
could only be
her
Edenic judgments.

from *The Atlantic*

At This Point My Confusion

◇   ◇   ◇

is an infomercial.
At the shop, it closes up many nights

like my parents had,
and turns back towards the unlit aisles

the way a person might turn to a choir and shrug.
A troubling choir.

Someone is asking if I'm ready,
and I'm on the couch folding these tiny pants.

I'm like a mule on a gondola, I say to my wife,
taking off a shoe with a lot of help.

Like an aristocrat on a riding mower, she says,
removing a sock.

A squirrel on an escalator, I nod, offering limited resistance.

My wife is sympathetic, smart, and beautiful.

You've come a long way, she says,
surely thinking of someone else.

from *Bennington Review*

Reasons for Staying

◊   ◊   ◊

October leaves coming down, as if called.

Morning fog through the wildrye beyond the train tracks.

A cigarette. A good sweater. On the sagging porch. While the family sleeps.

That I woke at all & the hawk up there thought nothing of its wings.

That I snuck onto the page while the guards were shitfaced on codeine.

That I read my books by the light of riotfire.

That my best words came farthest from myself & it's awesome.

That you can blow a man & your voice speaks through his voice.

Like Jonah through the whale.

Because a blade of brown rye, multiplied by thousands, makes a purple field.

Because this mess I made I made with love.

Because they came into my life, these ghosts, like something poured.

Because crying, believe it or not, did wonders.

Because my uncle never killed himself—but simply died, on purpose.

Because I made a promise.

That the McDonald's arch, glimpsed from the 2 am rehab window off Chestnut, was enough.

That mercy is small but the earth is smaller.

Summer rain hitting Peter's bare shoulders.

The *ptptptptptptpt* of it.

Because I stopped apologizing into visibility.

Because this body is my last address.

Because right now, just before morning, when it's blood-blue & the terror incumbent.

Because the sound of bike spokes heading home at dawn was unbearable.

Because the hills keep burning in California.

Through red smoke, singing. Through the singing, a way out.

Because only music rhymes with music.

The words I've yet to use: timothy grass, jeffrey pine, celloing, cocksure, light-lusty, midnight-green, gentled, water-thin, lord (as verb), russet, pewter, lobotomy.

The night's worth of dust on his upper lip.

Barnjoy on the cusp of winter.

The broken piano under a bridge in Windsor that sounds like footsteps when you play it.

The Sharpied sign outside the foreclosed house:

SEEKING CAT FRIEND. PLEASE KNOCK FOR KAYLA.

The train whistle heard through an opened window after a nightmare.

My mother, standing at the mirror, putting on blush before heading to chemo.

Sleeping in the back seat, leaving the town that broke me, whole.

Early snow falling from a clear, blushed sky.

As if called.

from *Harper's*

"In a dark time, the eye begins to see"

◇　◇　◇

The night hung
like a black anvil
over the treetops
when we started the fire
with a blue tipped match
and sat back to watch
darkness gather
around the flames
like children
drawn to fireflies
in an open hand.
When we looked
past the flames
all was a curtain
of mystery and ignorance,
so we poked the pit
with pointed sticks
and watched the wild
sparks scramble up
the canopy, a spiral
staircase of glints
chasing astral ancestors.
When we turned
our backs, the shadows
slunk into the woods

and disappeared among
the whispering leaves.
The moon was a fat spider
dangling from a black ceiling
and the barns were red
because the stars were dead.
We held our breath and
heard the whole forest sigh—
then a midnight peal of bells
unlocked the dread silence
and left us wondering
if this was the end
we'd dreamed of or
the beginning of the end
we couldn't afford
to see in the light.

from *jubilat*

ROBERT WHITEHEAD

Hi, How Are You

◇   ◇   ◇

HI
HOW
ARE YOU
DOING TODAY
& WHEN DO YOU
THINK IT WILL END?
SOMETIMES I'M A MAN
BUT THE TRICK IS TO LET
THE FEELING PASS WITHOUT
IT HARMING YOU. WHEN I LEFT
HOME TODAY I LEFT A FEELING LIKE
WHY BE ALIVE. I ASK THE QUESTION &
COMMIT MYSELF TO THE ANSWER WHERE
I AM NOT EATING MY OWN TAIL. HI I STILL FEAR
I WILL EAT MY OWN TAIL. AT THE NEUROCHEMICAL
LEVEL, EUPHORIA IS A LANGUAGE & AS SUCH HAS THE
POTENTIAL TO BECOME UNTRANSLATABLE. CALENDULA
USED TO BE MY MAINSTAY WHEN I NEEDED A YELLOW SHOCK
& SO I WOULD TURN LEFT AT THE STOP LIGHT DOWN THE BLOCK
& SAY HI TO THE CALENDULA, WHICH COULD MEAN, IN LATIN, THEY
SAY, LITTLE WEATHER-GLASS OR LITTLE CLOCK. THE TRICK IS TO LEAN
INTO THEIR YELLOW AUDIENCE & BREATHE UNTIL ONE DAY THE FLOWERS
ALL WILT & ALL YOU HAVE IS HOW YOU CALLED TO THEM IN THE AFTERNOON.
HI MY LITTLE CALENDARS. ANOTHER DAY HAS PASSED I IMAGINED WOULD NOT.

from *The Massachusetts Review*

Elegy for the Gnat

◇　◇　◇

who drowned
in my two fingers,

denied the bitter
sweetness of a black-

berry and nearly
surrendered to the meat

of a melon, but considered,
mostly, the craft

of thirst or death
and tongued itself

goodbye. oh, gentleness.
oh, small brown float

of a life. what news
should I give your beloveds?

most of them having
followed the rinds,

which too,
though I often forget,

are edible. blame
this on my desire,

which only knows
a soft end. and because

I am hesitant to end a thing,
you've done it

for me.

from *Ploughshares*

Final Poem for My Father Misnamed in My Mouth

◊　◊　◊

Sunlight still holds you and gives
your shapelessness to every room.
By noon, the kitchen catches your hands,
misshapen sun rays. The windows
have your eyes. Taken from me,
your body. I reorder my life with
absence. You are everywhere now
where once I could not find you
even in your own body. Death means
everything has become
possible. I've been told I have
your ways, your laughter haunts my mother
from my mouth. Everything
is possible. Fatherlight
washes over the kitchen floor.
I try to hold a bit of kindness
for the dead and make of memory
a sponge to wash your corpse.
Your name is not *addict* or *sir*.
This is not a dream: you died
and were buried three times. Once,
after my birth. Again, against
your hellos shedding into closing doors,
your face a mask I placed over my face.
The final time, you beneath my feet. Was I

buried with you then? I will not call
what you had left anything
other than *gone* and *sweet perhaps*. I am
not your junior, but I
survived. I fell in love with being
your son. Now what? Possibility
was a bird I once knew. It had one wing.

from *The New Yorker*

ELIZABETH WILLIS

What Else in Art Do You Pay For

◊   ◊   ◊

for CAConrad

To just sit down
is so much with you
No one seems to pick up
other people's garbage
but we do, all that
meaning under the surface
of the dirty white collar
Pick up pick up pick up
I'm calling you, I'm
the garbage now, the wall
what all of refuse, I try
not to refuse anything
except death
which I refuse with all my
aching Hank'd up heart
Have you read the letters
he wrote his mother
from the road
This shape is like my state
of mind when I think
of his heart aching
in the dumbest material
no matter what he strapped against it

Fire can't touch
a cold cold heart, it's blue
is black is green already
speaking to the brain
in any way it can
to ask forgiveness
My friend, I see the glitter
in your wounds
There isn't a single word
for what I want to say
To be loving anyone
is to abhor all harm
I don't know how to show you
the tree that saved my life
or whose reflected light
comes through the mouth
of the crystal you brought me
from the dirty patient earth

from *Bennington Review*

First, Chill

◊   ◊   ◊

This year I did not love the first snow,
took no joy from the clean whiteness

masking the contours of my yard,
the last leaves stripped from the weeping beech

to reveal its looping undercarriage,
the ground hardened underfoot

as the world froze in late November.
I have secretly admired the first hard frost

killing the garden, putting an end
to its many failures, the beetles and rusts

finally put to death, and which are hard
not to see as moral judgments

on my insufficient diligence.
This year I put on the woolens,

banked the stove with oak and elm,
watched the snow feather down

on the spruce, the grass still green under white,
and I felt an uncommon dread

for the inward turn that usually marks these days
that end in early nights at home

with their firelit contemplations,
the bright privacy of the lamp

encircling the pages of an open book.
I wanted more—not of summer,

with its swampy air and the nighttime
amphibian whir, but of autumn

with its metallic skies swept with clouds,
of the promise of something about to end,

but not yet taken away.
Above the Catskills, the peaks are veiled

in a cloud of snow. This is where
I think my dead have gone—

my father and Lucie and John—the dead
being impervious to cold,

having left their bodies with us to cherish,
but also to bury and to burn.

I imagine them as they wander the high peaks,
rippling like figures underwater,

like figures one dreams and forgets,
a shape drawn and erased

so only the pencil's impress remains.
Now that they are frozen

I know they are truly dead.
Let me let them go

I pray to the God of Nothingness
who rules those icy, bluestone peaks,

who hides the world of the living
underneath his coat of snow.

He has taken them from me
and now I will them, coldly, to go.

from *The Cortland Review*

Spark Theory

◇ ◇ ◇

Things flow one thing to another.
A hearse pulls up and idles.
Some plywood makes a peep.
Dark shapes in the doorway can't be helped.
It's not an insufficiency of electricity
that we need worry about, the stuff's
just bouncing off the streets.
The hearse is yellow with pollen.
The hearse almost covered with snow.
There is always this flow, rowboats,
marriages, upside down rainbows
of spilled gasoline. Here comes
a strange mailman, here comes
a chihuahua chewing a rubber band.
Here comes otherness in a flimsy dress.
A bird flies into a cotton tree,
a love letter crammed in a mannikin's head,
what she said that day by the water
with the ashes making their arabesques.
Simultaneously not being here yet
being nowhere else, occasions
for evaporation, perfumes of
the incinerated instance, a man carried
from his own house in pieces.
Like a harp.

from *Conduit*

Chris Martin Sings "Shiver" & I Shiver: A Poem for Madam Vice President

◇ ◇ ◇

This poem isn't for Coldplay or Rock 'n Roll or the Honda speakers or the 275
on-ramp to Dayton, OH on November 11. This poem isn't for Martin. Isn't for the way

his stool shook at First Avenue where I touched his foot, sweaty palmed & sweaty breasted,
before Apple, before Madison Square, & mouthed, *This Coldplay's gonna be big.* This poem

isn't for my grandfather, or his, *You'll never amount to anything*, gutturals, his, *You dirty
spic; waste of sperm*, pupils in spit at my brown body, my brown irises. This poem

isn't for the associate provost who pulled me into his office after the 2016 election,
saying, *We liberals will always be disadvantaged, Felicia, because we're unwilling to do horrid things*

to win, after asking me about my undocumented family, after asking, *You're Mexican right?*
This poem is not for his damaging white liberalism. This poem isn't for the playground

splashed with my blood after being punched in the face by the kid a grade above me & *Fuckin
Taco* in his saliva. Isn't for the asphalt, the snickers or that kid . . . all those kids.

This poem is for Kamala Harris. Madam Vice President Kamala Harris. This poem
is for my little brown body between my grandfather & the television, alert & still, not running

away, a demand to be seen. This poem is for my moon boots, thrift-store gems, & the tip
of the right boot in that kid's groin. This poem is for my mother who wrote nine children's

books in the '80s & not one accepted for publication. This poem is for *The Bear That Changes Colors, Glasses for Tommy Tiger, Betty Butterfly's Strange Mirror*, & the author's signature: *Linda*

Zamora. For the reason I became a poet—to write a poem to Madam Vice President—to say the word *possibility* & believe it. This poem is for the trillions of false litanies to women—*You*

can't X. Can't Y. Don't Z. Don't X. Cunt. You should Y. You should X. Fuck off. You don't belong. Don't get your panties in a bunch. Let me mansplain X. Relax. It's just a joke. You wanted this—may

this match burn these all down. This poem is for women. This poem is for Trans women. This poem is for Queer women. This poem is for Black women. This poem is for Brown

women. This poem is for Truth & Tubman & Parks. This poem is for Dove & hooks & Sanchez. This poem is for Anzaldúa, Baez, Cisneros. This poem is for women. This poem

is for Madam Vice President Kamala Harris. This poem is for how Martin sings "Shiver" & I shiver at your smile the night the electoral votes hit 290 blue. I see my face

in your smile—all the faces of history. I shiver for history. I shiver for my smile inside your smile. I shiver for the necessity of shivering long overdue, shivers of shivers.

This poem is for the ghazal. This poem is a ghazal because it's a world view. We stitch the stars down to earth now. We stitch the stars deep inside the soil of us, cells, salt-water

guts. We stitch with hair & wishbones for eyes, stitch until fingers bleed & then we stitch on top of the stitches. We taught ourselves to sew. We taught ourselves out of invisibility

the difference between the shadow cast & the body & yet part of the body & how a shadow means a body exists, a body in light. Step in, dear sisters. Step in.

from *Alaska Quarterly Review*

under the chiming bell

◇ ◇ ◇

under the chiming bell
I learn to move as ghosts do
after thirty-five years of belching
I finally qualify as a trophy
in the woods I am mostly small
~ insignificant ~
in love with nothing and no one
boredom is a kind of armor
capitalism no longer contagious
seeing with my own eyes
each raindrop ceasing to exist
still I fear birth as much as death
the non-consent of existence
will never be resolved in no lifetime
has anyone ever lived
through someone else's ending
or just me?
so weird being allowed to enter
not as a servant
but as a guest
the crudeness of patronage
all those childhood prayers
wasted essentially
in the end I was not too beautiful for this
failed to be much of an exception at all
at least I can still dream
to possess the kind of face
often inscribed into archways

mid-scream like a gargoyle with nothing
better to do
the holy don't need us
wretches of a different order
looking for someone or nothing
I was supposed to be staff
then everything changed
and it didn't even matter I was born wrong
will someone tell someone who I am
will someone please please tell me

from Poem-a-Day

CONTRIBUTORS' NOTES AND COMMENTS

ARIA ABER grew up in Germany, where she was born to Afghan parents. She is the author of *Hard Damage*, which won a Whiting Award and the Prairie Schooner Book Prize in Poetry. She is a Wallace Stegner Fellow at Stanford University.

RAYMOND ANTROBUS was born in London to an English mother and a Jamaican father. He is a Cave Canem Fellow and the author, most recently, of *The Perseverance* (Penned in the Margins [UK]/Tin House [US], 2018), and *All the Names Given* (Picador/Tin House, 2021) as well as a children's picture book, *Can Bears Ski?* (Walker Books 2021/ Candlewick Press, 2020). He is the 2019 recipient of the Ted Hughes Award as well as the Sunday Times/University of Warwick Young Writer of the Year Award, and he became the first poet to be awarded the Rathbone Folio Prize. *The Perseverance* was shortlisted for the Griffin Poetry Prize and the Forward Prize. He divides his time between London and New Orleans, and is an advocate for several D/deaf charities including Deaf Kidz International and National Deaf Children's Society.

Of "Text and Image," Antrobus writes: "After my wife, Tabitha, and I married in New Orleans I had to return to London to await our marriage visa. Then the pandemic happened and we weren't allowed to travel. We were separated for nine months and during that time we communicated through text messaging and voice notes, waking up every day and sharing our dreams. We'd have online dates and watch films. The raw material of the 'Text and Image' poems are from those online conversations and voice notes that sustained us and kept us connected through that time."

DARA BARROIS/DIXON was born in New Orleans, Louisiana, in 1949. Her new book is *Tolstoy Killed Anna Karenina* (Wave Books, 2022). Others include *In the Still of the Night* (2017), *You Good Thing* (2014), *Reverse Rapture* (2005), *Hat on a Pond* (2002), all from Wave Books, and *Voyages in English* (Carnegie Mellon University Press, 2001). Awards from the Lannan Foundation, *The American Poetry Review*, The Poetry Center, Guggenheim Foundation, National Endowment for the Arts, and Massachusetts Cultural Council have generously supported her work. Limited editions include *(X in Fix)* (2003) from Rain Taxi's brainstorm series, *Thru* (2019), *Two Poems* (2021) from Scram, and *Nine Poems* (2022) from Incessant Pipe. With James Tate, she rescued *The Lost Epic of Arthur Davidson Ficke*, published by Waiting for Godot Books (1999). She has been poet-in-residence at the University of Montana, University of Texas in Austin, Emory University, and the University of Utah, and held the 2005 Louis Rubin chair at Hollins University in Roanoke, Virginia. She lives and works in factory hollow in Western Massachusetts.

Of "Remembering," Barrois/Dixon writes: "Since April 2021 all poems I'm writing come in two parts, first part fourteen lines, second part prose, all one page. Often the prose parts include notes about what goes on before, during, and sometimes after the first parts come to be. In a way, many of the poems' prose parts contain what sometimes can be called stage directions and sometimes epilogue, afterword, or furtherance. The form the poems take has given me much pause, as of yet I'm unsure how to present it. This uncertainty has likely kept me writing them. It's been a strange intrigue how often one of these poems results from going down paths the daily *Hyperallergic* newsletter offers in its appended links. Not so with 'Remembering,' which resulted from being warned by a USPS truck that it was backing up and other things mentioned in the prose part of the poem. I suppose this constitutes a kind of ekphrastic, once or twice removed. I should probably thank *Hyperallergic*. I am, I do, I will."

E. C. BELLI was born in Switzerland in the early 1980s. She is the author of *A Sleep That Is Not Our Sleep* (Anhinga Press, 2022) and *Objects of Hunger* (Southern Illinois University Press, 2019). She is also the translator of *I, Little Asylum* by Emmanuelle Guattari (Semiotext(e),

2014) and *The Nothing Bird: Selected Poems by Pierre Peuchmaurd* (Oberlin College Press, 2013).

Of "Vows," Belli writes: "I ask forgiveness of the stones for this. They are, after all, *resistant* matter. Consider their impermeability, their weight and density, their beautiful conciseness as pebbles. Extrapolating on G. Bachelard's materialist *imagination activiste*, we might even find that a writing articulated by what could be termed a 'poetics of stone' offers itself as a potent form of resistance against raving or convulsively virulent discourses."

OLIVER BAEZ BENDORF was born in 1987 in Iowa City, Iowa. He is the author of *Advantages of Being Evergreen* (Cleveland State University Poetry Center, 2019) and *The Spectral Wilderness* (Kent State University Press, 2015). He has received a National Endowment for the Arts Fellowship for Poetry and the Betty Berzon Emerging Writer Award from the Publishing Triangle. He lives in Olympia, Washington.

Of "What the Dead Can Do," Bendorf writes: I drafted this poem in the classroom, while my undergraduate poetry students also wrote. (This was at Kalamazoo College, where I was teaching at the time.) I was responding in my notebook to the prompt from Dorianne Laux and Kim Addonizio to imagine, of the dead, 'What are their powers and limitations? What are their desires, fears, pleasures?' That class in late February 2020 was, though I didn't know it yet, one of the last times we'd meet on campus before the pandemic took hold, and took so much. Therefore, I offer this poem to all the newly dead whom we've lost, about whose powers and pleasures I must know nothing yet."

KRISTIN BOCK's second poetry collection, *Glass Bikini*, was published by Tupelo Press in 2021. Her first, *CLOISTERS*, won Tupelo Press's First Book Award and an Eric Hoffer da Vinci Eye Award. A Massachusetts Cultural Council Fellow, she holds an MFA in poetry from the University of Massachusetts, Amherst, where she teaches. She lives in western Massachusetts with her husband and together they restore liturgical art.

WILLIAM BREWER was born in West Virginia in 1989. He is the author of *The Red Arrow* (Alfred A. Knopf, 2022) and *I Know Your Kind* (Milkweed Editions, 2017). Formerly a Wallace Stegner Fellow, he is now a Jones Lecturer at Stanford University, and lives in Oakland.

Of "Anthony Bourdain," Brewer writes: "Growing up in a rural part of America, I craved to be anywhere but where I was, so when I discovered the first episode of Bourdain's first show in 2002, it was like discovering a portal leading to pretty much anywhere I could imagine. More importantly, I immediately recognized that whoever this person was, he was moving through the world in a way I should hope to do so, too, i.e., like a guest. I learned a great deal from his programs and found immense comfort in them, especially as I aged into my teens and twenties, during which time I also developed severe suicidal depression that left me feeling less like a guest on this earth and more like an intruder, no matter where I was or who I was with. Needless to say, his death by suicide was a shock. This poem came out of that."

JERICHO BROWN was born in Shreveport, Louisiana, in 1976 and lives in Atlanta, Georgia. His most recent book, *The Tradition* (Copper Canyon Press, 2019), won the Pulitzer Prize. He is also the author of *Please* (New Issues, 2008) and *The New Testament* (Copper Canyon, 2014).

Of "Inaugural," Brown writes: "I have my editor Michael Wiegers to thank for this poem. It was his idea that I write it. It gave me a way to say, 'God bless, America' in all the tones anyone ever could."

JAMES CAGNEY was born in Oakland, California, in 1968 and still lives there. Nomadic Press published his first book, *Black Steel Magnolias in the Hour of Chaos Theory*, which won the 2019 PEN Oakland Josephine Miles Award, and his James Laughlin Award–winning collection *MARTIAN: The Saint of Loneliness* in September 2022. Please visit JamesCagneyPoet.com.

Cagney writes: "During the stay-at-home order, I spent several weeks thinking and writing about friendships I had as a young man that couldn't be maintained. The friend featured in the poem 'Proof' was an outlier. Over the years, I've tried searching for him on social media, to no avail. He was a Bay Area poet whom I respected, though I don't remember us being close before that meal and afterward only occasionally running into him. I do recall that café having the best pancakes I'd ever eaten, and learning crepes were pretty much the same thing and they shouldn't be ordered together. Why we were talking about doctors instead of basketball or girls was my fault as at the time I was caretaker to my mother and grandfather. I held this memory for decades before it finally congealed into 'Proof.' People under a certain age won't know the mid-'60s sitcom *I Dream of Jeannie*, in which a single woman with magic powers lives (unmarried!) with a single man whom she calls, ahem, 'Master.' But the trivia shared in the poem is true: her bare midriff genie costume, now at the Smithsonian, created problems for TV executives and network censors. I knew of the belly-button issue, but recently learned the pants of her costume were darkened to keep her legs from being seen."

BILL CARTY was born in Maine in 1981 and now lives in Seattle. He is the author of *Huge Cloudy* (Octopus Books, 2019).

Of "Outer Lands," Carty writes: "I began this poem in the fall of 2018, when I was on a returning residency at the Fine Arts Work Center in Provincetown, where I'd been a fellow in 2013–14. I grew up in coastal Maine and now live in Seattle, a stone's throw from Puget Sound, and I'm always returning to the ocean in life and, apparently, poems. In this case, a chance encounter with a seal near Wood End lighthouse, near the very tip of Cape Cod, led to this meditation—parts real, parts imagined—on fear and futility, on nature and violence, and the way such experiences might be mediated through technology."

JENNIFER CHANG was born in New Jersey in 1976, and educated at the University of Chicago and the University of Virginia. She is the author of *The History of Anonymity* (University of Georgia Press, 2008) and *Some Say the Lark* (Alice James, 2017), which received the 2018 William Carlos Williams Award and was longlisted for the Julie Suk Award and the PEN Open Book Award. She cochairs the advisory board of Kundiman, is the poetry editor of the *New England Review*, and teaches creative writing at the University of Texas in Austin.

Of "The Innocent," Chang writes: "It's true that children like routine or, at least, mine do. In the early days of the pandemic our routine was, through necessity, atomized, planned down to mere minutes. After daybreak, after breakfast and morning chores, I'd take my children out back to our neighbor's yard to check the robin's nest and then head back in to sit in our respective corners with our respective screens. It was March in Washington, D.C., nearly spring, and we—my children, my neighbors, the animals among us—were acutely aware of what we did nearly every minute of the day, as if each of us were on a small stage. What were we looking at, looking for? This poem is an artifact of that time but also performs what we, as adults, were trying to do with time at our most vulnerable: to name it, contain it, frame it in a story that makes sense to someone, anyone, and hopefully ends well. We try to make time fit into the life we want for ourselves. We try. Even now, two years into the pandemic, the trying feels foolhardy but stricken equally with grief and hope. The only creature who isn't innocent here is the cat, who truly is terrible and kills countless birds and rodents in the alley behind our houses. His name is Cubby; watch out for him."

CATHY LINH CHE is a Vietnamese American writer born in Los Angeles in 1980. She is the author of *Split* (Alice James Books, 2014), winner of the Kundiman Poetry Prize, the Norma Farber First Book Award from the Poetry Society of America, and the Best Poetry Book Award from the Association of Asian American Studies. She has taught at the 92nd Street Y, New York University, Fordham University, Sierra Nevada College, and the Polytechnic University at NYU. She is working on a poetry manuscript, a creative nonfiction manuscript, and a short documentary, with director Christopher Radcliff, on her parents' experiences as refugees who played extras in *Apocalypse Now*. Currently a PhD student in English at Fordham University, she is executive director at Kundiman and lives on the traditional lands of the Lenape people.

Che writes: "'Marriage' is a poem that I was happy to write but embarrassed to share. I have been thinking more and more about what it means to reproduce ourselves—through art, through offspring— what it means to live, love, age, die, leave a legacy when our world is facing potential extinction. These anxieties feel clichéd, and I certainly don't want my life and desires to feel clichéd, but when I have read this poem out loud, I saw and felt others' recognition, and that meant a lot to me, to open up and to feel less alone."

TIANA CLARK was born in Los Angeles in 1984. She is the author of *I Can't Talk About the Trees Without the Blood* (University of Pittsburgh Press, 2018) and *Equilibrium* (Bull City Press, 2016).

Of "Broken Sestina Reaching for Black Joy," Clark writes: "I believe writing in form is a way to reckon with obsession, while breaking a form is a way to find freedom from restraint. I wanted to disrupt, needle, and subvert the sestina's predetermined pattern for repetition by toggling order and chaos, manipulating the repetends to mimic my mind responding to the immediate world around me. In doing so, the poem becomes a pendulum oscillating the trajectory between Black pain and Black bliss."

MICHAEL EARL CRAIG was born in Dayton, Ohio, in 1970. His most recent book is *Woods and Clouds Interchangeable* (Wave Books, 2019). A recent poet laureate for the state of Montana, he lives near Livingston where he shoes horses for a living.

Of "Preparing for Sleep," Craig writes: "This poem is of one of my 'insomnia poems' where I can't sleep and I'm staring at the dark ceiling and a line or an image comes to mind. If one thing leads to another, and it's obvious I won't be sleeping any time soon, I'll give in and sneak off into another room and start writing. Almost always when I do this the writing comes very quickly and naturally. I'm pretty sure with this one I got out of bed when I got to Old Ironsides."

LAURA CRONK was born in 1977 in New Castle, Indiana. She is the author most recently of *Ghost Hour* (Persea Books, 2020). She teaches writing and pedagogy classes at The New School in New York.

Of "Today: What Is Sexy," Cronk writes: "I remember the moment I began to write this poem. It was June in New York, hot but not too hot, and I was in the audience of a Lydia Davis reading. I think she was reading from *Can't and Won't*. Suddenly the images from my own day felt fresh and alive in a totally new way."

DIANA MARIE DELGADO is the literary director of the University of Arizona Poetry Center and has worked for more than twenty years in not-for-profits focused on advancing social justice and the arts. Her first collection, *Tracing the Horse* (BOA Editions, 2019), was a *New York*

Times Noteworthy Pick and follows the coming-of-age of a young Chicana trying to make sense of who she is amid a family and community weighted by violence and addiction. She has an MFA from Columbia University and has received grants from the National Endowment for the Arts, Hedgebrook, Bread Loaf, and the Arizona Commission on the Arts. She was born in West Covina, California, in 1975.

Delgado writes: "I've often thought about how much more truthful stream of consciousness reads for me. It's also forgiving of the many leaps and bridges that occur back and forth in time, building an immediacy and intimacy that I personally enjoy. I had that in mind while drafting 'Separate but Umbilical Situations Relating to My Father,' which began as a much longer poem (a tome in fact!) that I condensed with the idea that I would discover a last line that would stop the poem in its tracks. I love the idea of something wild and loose that comes to a place of rest. The editing took years of simmering, but was worthwhile; the poem's ending, for me, surfaced a sentiment about my dad that I otherwise would never have considered."

MATTHEW DICKMAN was born in Portland, Oregon, in the summer of 1975. He is the author of *All-American Poem* (APR/Copper Canyon Press, 2008), *Mayakovsky's Revolver* (W. W. Norton, 2012), *Wonderland* (Norton, 2018), and *Husbandry* (Norton, 2022). He lives in Portland with his sons, Hamza and Owen.

Of "Goblin," Dickman writes: "Something I am always struck by but not always mindful of (and have not always put into practice) is just how defenseless children are against their parents. Babies smell good and are cute, toddlers begin to look a little like their parents, grade schoolers might mimic their parents, but a child's safety really all depends on the adult, on the mom or dad or caretaker not being terrible. Of course the child has no control over *that* complicated gamble. Inside any parent the opportunity for great kindness or cruelty is equal. That goes for me, too. And anyway, most parents are still children in many real ways and often injured children at that. It was thinking about this imbalance of power and the realization, during some pretend-time playing with my youngest son Owen, that I could hurt him anytime I wanted to, that the poem 'Goblin' first started manifesting. What was most surprising to me about this particular experience playing 'goblin' with Owen was not how much I loved the feeling of soothing him after he got upset but the strange and embarrassing thought that came into my head after: If I ever wanted to have that feeling of soothing him, of being the person who made him feel better, all I had to do was make him feel sad or scared. I want so much for my sons to be safe, to be safe in this world, safe even from their own father or mother. I want the child I once was to have been safer. Being a kid is hard. Being a parent is hard. But it's our job, not the child's, to make sure goblins don't eat them."

TISHANI DOSHI was born in Madras, India, in 1975. She publishes poetry, essays, and fiction. For fifteen years she worked as the lead dancer of the Chandralekha dance company in Madras. Her most recent novel, *Small Days and Nights* (W. W. Norton, 2020), was short-listed for the RSL Ondaatje Prize and was a *New York Times Book Review* Editors' Choice. She is a visiting associate professor at New York University, Abu Dhabi. *A God at the Door*, her fourth full-length collection of poetry, was published by Copper Canyon Press in 2021, and was shortlisted for the Forward Poetry Prize in the UK.

Of "Advice for Pliny the Elder, Big Daddy of Mansplainers," Doshi writes: "This poem is a rejoinder to Pliny the Elder who in his encyclopedic *Naturalis Historia* stated his belief that menstrual blood was so dangerous that a mere drop could kill bees, cause seeds in gardens to dry up, make a man's sword useless, and destroy whole fields. Pliny the Elder had a sister who is believed to have first seen the smoke of Vesuvius erupting. He went off to investigate and/or to help friends who lived nearby. The details are unclear, but we know he perished there."

CAMILLE T. DUNGY was born in Colorado in 1972. She is the author of four collections of poetry, most recently *Trophic Cascade* (Wesleyan University Press, 2017), winner of the Colorado Book Award, and the essay collection *Guidebook to Relative Strangers: Journeys into Race, Motherhood, and History* (W. W. Norton, 2017), finalist for the National Book Critics Circle Award. She has edited three anthologies, including *Black Nature: Four Centuries of African American Nature Poetry* (University of Georgia Press, 2009). Her forthcoming book is *Soil: The History of a Black Mother's Garden* (Simon & Schuster). She has received the 2021 Academy of American Poets Fellowship, a Guggenheim Fellowship, an American Book Award, and NEA Fellowships in both poetry and prose. With her husband and daughter, she lives in Colorado, where she is a University Distinguished Professor at Colorado State University.

Of "Let Me," Dungy writes: "In the midst of the fire season out here in the West, while working on my new book, *Soil: The History of a Black Mother's Garden*, I wrote some notes about a brick I gathered years ago from the rubble of an old warehouse I once visited in a historic southeastern American city. Writing about the brick triggered memories I'd pushed aside for many years. As those memories tumbled out, so did this poem."

Safia Elhillo, born in 1990, is the author of *The January Children* (University of Nebraska Press, 2017), *Girls That Never Die* (One World/Random House, 2022), and the novel in verse *Home Is Not a Country* (Make Me a World/Random House, 2021). She has won a Ruth Lilly and Dorothy Sargent Rosenberg Fellowship from the Poetry Foundation, a Cave Canem award, and a Wallace Stegner Fellowship from Stanford University.

Of "Ode to Sudanese Americans," Elhillo writes: "I wanted to make an offering to my communities, to the vibrant diasporic communities that raised me and named me and taught me. I was newly relocated to California when I wrote this poem, and realized how much I'd taken this proximity to my community for granted in D.C. and in New York. I miss them, my friends, my friendcousins, my hundred siblings, so I made them this poem in hopes that it will make them laugh a little, and let them know that I am thinking of them."

Born in 1994, Shangyang Fang grew up in Chengdu, China. A Wallace Stegner Fellow at Stanford University, he is the author of the poetry collection *Burying the Mountain* (Copper Canyon Press, 2021).

Of "A Bulldozer's American Dream," Fang writes: "It was earliest months when COVID-19 hit, and quarantine became a way to live. The construction site beside my apartment remained loud and busy, even on weekends. I couldn't read or write. One afternoon, I watched the workers from my balcony for a long time. At night, the rain came, a bulldozer standing alone in the jagged field. It looked like someone's abandoned pet. I was stirred by this image. I started writing."

VIEVEE FRANCIS was born in San Angelo, Texas, in 1963. Her books of poetry include *Blue-Tail Fly* (Wayne State University Press, 2006), *Horse in the Dark* (winner of the Cave Canem Northwestern University Poetry Prize for a second collection; Northwestern University Press, 2016), *Forest Primeval* (winner of the Hurston Wright Legacy Award and the 2017 Kingsley Tufts Poetry Award; TriQuarterly, 2015), and *The Shared World* (Northwestern, 2022). Her work has appeared in five previous editions of *The Best American Poetry* and in *Angles of Ascent: A Norton Anthology of Contemporary African American Poetry*. She has been a poet-in-residence for the Alice Lloyd Scholars Program at the University of Michigan. In 2009 she received a Rona Jaffe Writer's Award, and in 2010, a Kresge Fellowship. A former associate editor of *Callaloo*, she is an associate professor of English and creative writing at Dartmouth College in Hanover, New Hampshire.

FORREST GANDER, born in the Mojave Desert (Barstow), lives in California. A translator/writer with degrees in geology and literature, he received the Pulitzer Prize, Best Translated Book Award, and fellowships from the Library of Congress, Guggenheim, and United States Artists foundations. His book *Twice Alive* (New Directions, 2021) focuses on human and ecological intimacies.

Of "Sea: Night Surfing in Bolinas," Gander writes: "Who are we once those with whom we've spent so much of our lives, those who shared the memories by which we recognize and define ourselves, have died or are gone? In what sense does our thinking about them make them present again? My life-partner died unexpectedly, but I feel her company, her witness, in every conscious act of my life without her. Being submerged in the sea, listening to an alien world, struck me as an experience not unlike being submerged in grief or love and listening into the beyond of what we call our time and death-bound lives."

LOUISE GLÜCK was born in New York City in 1943. Among many honors for her work are a 1993 Pulitzer Prize for *The Wild Iris*, a 2014

National Book Award for *Faithful and Virtuous Night*, and the Nobel Prize for Literature in 2020. Her most recent book is *Winter Recipes from the Collective* (Farrar, Straus and Giroux, 2021). She teaches at Yale University and Stanford University, and was the guest editor of *The Best American Poetry 1993*.

APRIL GOLDMAN was born in 1984 and raised in Houston, Texas. Her interests include ecopoetics and ecofeminism, disability studies and mental illness, nonhuman animal rights, and her dogs Lloyd and Pinky. She earned an MFA in poetry from the University of Houston and is working on her first collection. Say hello on Instagram @aprileli.

Of "Into the Mountains," Goldman writes: "I love collage as a writing process. I wrote this poem by pulling lines from several years' worth of my writing notebooks. The first line in the poem came from an elegy I tried to write for my teacher, the second line came from a fragment about waking up in bed next to my beloved, etc. Each line came from some other writing project that failed, and I love the fact that even failed poems can be full of seeds for future poems."

PAUL GUEST was born in Chattanooga, Tennessee, in 1974. He was an undergraduate at the University of Tennessee and received his Master of Fine Arts from Southern Illinois University. He has published several books of poetry, including *The Resurrection of the Body and the Ruin of the World* (New Issues, 2003), *Notes for My Body Double* (University of Nebraska Press, 2007), *My Index of Slightly Horrifying Knowledge* (Ecco, 2008), and *Because Everything Is Terrible* (Diode Editions, 2018). His memoir *One More Theory About Happiness* (Ecco, 2010) was a selection of the Barnes & Noble Discover Great New Writers Program. He has taught at the University of Virginia, Agnes Scott College, University of West Georgia, and University of Alabama. He is a Whiting Award winner and a Guggenheim Fellow.

Of "Theories of Revenge," Guest writes: "When I was twelve years old, I broke my neck in a bicycle accident. Thrown over the handlebars headfirst, I was paralyzed from the injury to my spinal cord. In that instant, many different weights fell on me. One was the knowledge that I'd never walk again. Another, nearly as immediate, was that my life would never again really be mine. I would always live in the long shadows of my parents' grief, though they never spoke of it to me. I remember one hot afternoon, a few months later, I was on a therapy mat in a rehabilitation hospital when a curly-haired boy was wheeled in. Until then, I'd been the youngest patient and he was younger than I was. I hated him, a little bit. I wanted my suffering to remain unique. Later, I'd learn his parents had signed a Do Not Resuscitate order, should he ever stop breathing. I don't know what happened to him. In the years since, I have resisted, often enough, the urge to write more explicitly about my body, my disability—I say it's mine, as though catastrophe is ever neatly contained. In this poem, I tried to imagine the weight of the truth."

JALYNN HARRIS was born in Baltimore, Maryland, in 1995. She is a poet, educator, and book designer. She has an MFA in Creative Writing & Design, as well as a BA in Linguistics.

Of "The Life of a Writer," Harris writes: "Deep inside the jaws of the pandemic, I'd found myself chewed up and swallowed by unending loneliness. The morning I wrote this poem, I'd completely given myself over to looking outside the window of my longing; I was writing love poems. What I saw was a streetlight. A man-made object that dared to mimic the elegance of the moon. This symbol of light was just enough for me to know that all the love my heart longed for was not as out of reach as I'd been made to feel. That if the streetlight could derive its meaning from the moon, then the longing I pressed out of my pen was also bringing me closer and closer to something more real and more exciting than I could ever imagine. How horrifying! And how energizing to be completely alone yet comforted by creating a poem: a record of where I was and a contract for where I was going."

TERRANCE HAYES was born in Columbia, South Carolina, in 1971. His most recent publications include *American Sonnets for My Past and Future Assassin* (Penguin, 2018), and *To Float in the Space Between: Drawings and Essays in Conversation with the Life and Work of Etheridge Knight* (Wave Books, 2018). He was the guest editor of *The Best American Poetry 2014*.

Of "What Would You Ask the Artist?" Hayes writes, "This is a part of an ekphrastic DIY sestina triptych. Each sestina tows a sort of associative, tripling, spilling broken envoi."

BRENDA HILLMAN was born in Tucson, Arizona, in 1951. She has edited and coedited numerous volumes of poetry and prose, and is the author of twelve collections of poetry from Wesleyan University Press, including *Extra Hidden Life, among the Days* (2018) and *In a Few Minutes Before Later* (2022). She is a Chancellor Emerita at the Academy of American Poets, teaches at Saint Mary's College of California, and directs the Poetry Week at Community of Writers.

Of ":::[to the voice of the age]:::," Hillman writes: "This piece is from a series of poems called 'The Sickness & the World Soul' written during the first year of the pandemic. The numbers refer to the numbers of cases when I began the poem and when I completed it. It is dedicated to Geoffrey G. O'Brien."

NOOR HINDI was born in Amman, Jordan, in 1995. She is a Palestinian American poet and reporter, and a 2021 Ruth Lilly and Dorothy Sargent Rosenberg Fellow. Follow her on Twitter @MyNrhindi.

MAJOR JACKSON was born in Philadelphia in 1968 and is the author of *A Beat Beyond: The Selected Prose of Major Jackson* (University of Michigan Press, 2022). His latest volume of poetry is *The Absurd Man* (W. W. Norton, 2020). He teaches at Vanderbilt University, where he is the Gertrude Conaway Vanderbilt Chair in the Humanities. Jackson was the guest editor of *The Best American Poetry 2019*.

Of "Ode to Everything," Jackson writes: "Odes never go out of style. I have a simple heart; I surrender to all forms of beauty: here, in this poem, friends, nature, and food. We can never praise enough, especially the selfless among us. I recently arrived at a moment in my life when I was willing to forgive, and so, what initially looked like failures or cruelties in my past, I view differently today as occasions to acknowledge the inevitability of my journey. And thus, I want to write an ode to everything."

BRIONNE JANAE is a poet and teaching artist living in Brooklyn. They are the author of *Blessed Are the Peacemakers*, which won the 2020 Cave Canem Northwestern University Press Poetry Prize, and *After Jubilee* (BOAAT Press, 2017). Brionne is the recipient of the St. Botoloph Emerging Artist award, a Hedgebrook Alum, and proud Cave Canem

Fellow. Brionne is the co-host of the podcast *The Slave Is Gone* along-side poet Jericho Brown and Rogue Scholar Aífe Murray. Off the page they go by Breezy.

RODNEY JONES was born in 1950 in Hartselle, Alabama. He is the author of eleven books, including *Transparent Gestures* (Ecco, 1989), winner of the National Book Critics Circle Award; *Things That Happen Once* (Houghton Mifflin Harcourt, 1996); *Elegy for the Southern Drawl* (Ecco, 1999); *Salvation Blues* (Houghton Mifflin, 2006), which won the Kingsley Tufts Prize and was shortlisted for the Griffin International Poetry Prize; and *Village Prodigies* (Mariner Books, 2017), a hybrid poem-novel. He has taught at Southern Illinois University at Carbondale and the Warren Wilson low residency MFA program, served as the Mary Rodgers Field Distinguished University Professor at DePauw University, and as the Visiting Elliston Poet at the University of Cincinnati. He lives in New Orleans.

Jones writes: "In 'How Much I Loved This Life,' I build a literary contraption to hold a night terror that pops up so regularly I should be slipping it table scraps and training it to heel, but no; my inner child is trolled, grasped, and at the point of maximum angst, expresses itself with woe. Whether this night terror has a den in my DNA, the scarifying, fundamentalist visions of eternal damnation that were in the air around me as a child, or cold war rhetoric, it's a miracle that I'm not QAnon."

LAURA KASISCHKE was born in Lake Charles, Louisiana, in 1961. She has published eleven collections of poetry, most recently *Lightning Falls in Love* (Copper Canyon Press, 2021), and eleven works of fiction.

Of "When a bolt of lightning falls in love," Kasischke writes: "The poem began as some late-night jottings in a notebook, written while—as the poem indicates—in a motel room. Then I lost the notebook. But I recalled the title and the first lines and the general inspiration, which was the consideration of the lightning storm outside my rather dingy motel near a freeway, the passage of time, the trip I was attempting to take to visit my son on the other side of the Atlantic Ocean, and the various properties of lightning, love, sex, and obligation (past, present, and future; ongoing and ending), not necessarily in that order. As I tend to do, I went on and on and on in my associations, in a new notebook, which I knew one day I'd also lose, like the other one—but this time I moved the poem from the handwritten to the computer, right away, and then I pared it down to the lines I felt were the ones that best moved from the title to the message I felt the poem was trying to send to me by the end."

LAURA KOLBE, born in Bethlehem, Pennsylvania, in 1986, is a poet, physician, and medical ethicist. Her debut poetry collection, *Little Pharma*, won the Agnes Lynch Starrett Prize and was published in 2021 by the University of Pittsburgh Press. She has received support from MacDowell and the Key West Literary Seminar. She lives in New York City.

Of "Buried Abecedary for Intensive Care," Kolbe writes: "My beloved 'day job' as a doctor rightly requires a degree of self-effacement and a relinquishment of the expectation of control. I am not fully at liberty; I speak an argot not my native tongue; the contingencies of illness steer my thought and mood. They tell me where things end. This is the only abecedary poem I've written, but its strictures struck me as right when trying to get at the swept-along feeling of working in an intensive-care unit, as I did during my training as a medical resident. By submitting to the arbitrary constraint of the alphabet's order, I am reliving the ways in which neither clinicians nor patients fully self-govern when the extremes of illness rule the boundaries of what happens."

JASON KOO is a second-generation Korean American poet, educator, editor, and nonprofit director. Born in New York City in 1976 and raised in Cleveland, Ohio, he is the author of three full-length collections of poetry: *More Than Mere Light* (Prelude Books, 2018), *America's Favorite Poem* (C&R Press, 2014; Brooklyn Arts Press, 2020) and *Man on Extremely Small Island* (C&R, 2009; Brooklyn Arts, 2020). He is also the author of the limited-edition chapbook & cassette tape *Sunset Park* (Frontier Slumber, 2017) and coeditor of the *Brooklyn Poets Anthology* (Brooklyn Arts & Brooklyn Poets, 2017). He has won fellowships from the National Endowment for the Arts, Vermont Studio Center, and New York State Writers Institute. An associate teaching professor of English at Quinnipiac University, Koo is the founder and executive director of Brooklyn Poets and creator of the Bridge (poetsbridge.org), a networking site connecting poets and mentors. For his work with Brooklyn Poets, Koo was named one of the "100 Most Influential People in Brooklyn Culture" by *Brooklyn Magazine*.

Koo writes: "For a long time I thought that I would never be in *Best American Poetry*. Because of my name, my style, the length of my poems—who knows why. You tell yourself these things don't matter, that just writing good poems is enough, but then a White man sneaks in under an appropriated Asian name and it's like one giant smirk at your whole existence. So I'm enormously grateful to Matthew Zapruder for recognizing my work and making me feel legitimately visible, for believing this poem was good enough to merit all these pages, when there were so many other good (and much shorter) poems he could have chosen instead. I'm also grateful to the editors at *Copper Nickel*—Nicky Beer, Brian Barker, and Wayne Miller—for publishing this long poem in a print journal, where every page is so costly (especially for a journal that pays contributors by the page), and giving Zapruder a chance to see it."

DEBORAH LANDAU is the author of five collections of poetry, including *Soft Targets* (Copper Canyon Press), winner of the 2019 Believer Book Award, and *Skeletons*, forthcoming from Copper Canyon Press in 2023. She is a professor and the director of the Creative Writing Program at New York University.

Of "Skeletons," Landau writes: "These linked poems are from my book-length series *Skeletons*. I've rarely written in form, but the acrostics were a way to keep writing during the early days of the pandemic, locked down in Brooklyn while the ambulances sirened by. It was a profoundly destabilizing season, but each eight-word list set off a generative momentum that made it possible to write into the chaos and overwhelm of that time. Later I threaded a series of 'Flesh' poems through the book—some Eros to counterpoint the Thanatos."

LI-YOUNG LEE is a U.S. citizen of Chinese descent born in 1957 in Jakarta, Indonesia. His books include, from BOA Editions: *Rose* (1986), *The City in Which I Love You* (1990), and *Book of My Nights*

(2001); and from W. W. Norton: *Behind My Eyes* (2000) and *The Undressing* (2018).

Lee writes: "As I try to say something meaningful about 'Big Clock,' I realize what a Quixotic errand my mind embarked upon when I set out to write that poem. For not a single question about Time and Death and their relationship to Eternity, questions that drove me to sit down and try to write, got answered. I'm just as confused now as I was before I wrote the poem, maybe even more so. Strangely, however, after having written the thing, I'm now more comfortable in my confounded state, where before I was losing sleep. Here are the grains of sand that itched me and robbed me of that most fragrant flower in the garden, sleep:

First grain: From my earliest years of sojourning with my parents and siblings as refugees looking for a country to call home, there is a memory of a giant stopped clock in a train station. One brother claimed it was a train station in Indonesia. He's buried there. Another brother said it was actually our father's pocket watch. Yet another brother said it was a station in either Japan or Hong Kong. Both of them died young. Of the three siblings who survived, my sister says it was a train station in China, my brother says Seattle, and I can't tell our mother's and father's faces from the face of a clock, ever since death had its way with them.

Second grain: Years ago, a dear friend said to me, 'I live in Eternity all the time now.' Indeed, whenever I was in her presence, I also felt I was living in eternity, and that the world of human time, smeared by profit traders and power brokers and influence peddlers, was unreal. But death had its way with my friend, too. And yet, she also said to me, 'You're not paying attention, Li-Young. Eternity isn't more Time. Time multiplied is still Time.'

Third grain: My childhood feels like it lasted an eternity, yet no longer than any dawn, any dusk.

Fourth grain: Emily Dickinson said something like, 'No Heaven-at-last for me. But Heaven-all-along.' I love that so much. Did she mean, 'No happy-place-at-last for me. But happy-place-all-along'? No way she was that stupid or shallow. Did she mean, 'No Eternity-at-last for me. But Eternity-all-along'? And what would that mean? That we've been living in Eternity all along? That Time is another face of Eternity? Maybe, looking out through Death's eyes, Eternity looks like Time. Did she mean, 'No being-with-God-at-last for me. But being-with-God-all-along'? And what if that were true, that I'm with-God-all-along? All of my discursiveness sounds stupid and shallow next to the depth of Dickinson's testimony.

Fifth grain: Where do trauma, war, displacement, indeed, suffering altogether, fit into Eternity? Or Heaven? Is suffering eternal? Am I using 'eternal' to mean 'more time' in that previous question? Is suffering a feature of Heaven or is it a bug? Can I write a poem that simultaneously enacts both faces, Time and Eternity? Can I make a poem that is both a depiction of Heaven and Earth? If what mathematicians claim is true, that there are different magnitudes of infinities, can the same be said about Eternity? Are there different orders of Eternities? Who makes up these questions? Did God slap a poster on my back that reads, 'Keep this guy running'? Why do these questions needle me? Maybe I should get a job and earn some wages.

Sixth grain: All movement is only possible against a fixity. The body can only move forward by a foot's pushing against the earth. I can only stand up from my seat by pushing against the earth and the chair. If Time moves, what is the hidden fixity it moves against?"

DANA LEVIN was born in Los Angeles, California, in 1965 and grew up in the Mojave Desert. She is the author of five books of poetry, most recently *Now Do You Know Where You Are* (Copper Canyon Press, 2022), a Lannan Literary Selection. She has received fellowships and awards from the National Endowment for the Arts, PEN, and the Library of Congress, as well as the Lannan, Rona Jaffe, Whiting, and Guggenheim Foundations. She is Distinguished Writer in Residence at Maryville University in Saint Louis.

Of "January Garden," Levin writes: "The poem is a chronicle of two primary activities that help me write: listening and walking. By listening, I mean specifically to messages that cross from the underground well of the psyche (or is it the outer-spatial realm of the Muse?) into consciousness as I wake up. By walking, I mean walking, often in Tower Grove Park here in Saint Louis. I was walking there one day in winter, mind nattering on, when suddenly: that title! That had come with me out of sleep! And then, there was the young woman at the picnic table, writing with her plastic novelty pen in the shape of a bone. The title and the woman writing spoke to each other. Then I knew to go back to my recent cache of hypnagogic messages, because the rest of the poem was in there, a poem about listening and walking and seeing and writing: a poem about practicing mercy in this murderous world."

ADA LIMÓN was born in Sonoma, California, in 1976. She is the author of six books of poetry including *The Hurting Kind* (Milkweed Editions, 2022).

Of "My Father's Mustache," Limón writes: "During the early months of the pandemic, my father sent me a photograph of himself from the early '70s. Something about that photograph deeply affected me. There was such a freedom and confidence in his gesture. At a time when I could not see him, could not see anyone, I was struck by how much I missed everything. I wanted to honor my father, but also honor that feeling of missing."

IRÈNE MATHIEU was born in Washington, D.C., in 1987. She is a pediatrician, writer, and author of the poetry collections *the galaxy of origins* (dancing girl press, 2014), *orogeny* (Trembling Pillow Press, 2017), and *Grand Marronage* (Switchback Books, 2019). Her fourth collection, *milk tongue*, is forthcoming from Deep Vellum Press in 2023.

Of "the junkyard galaxy knocks," Mathieu writes: "I wrote this poem after being mystified by my dog's habit of staring at things I can't see—in the darkened window of my apartment at the time (the neighbor's TV referenced in the poem being invisible from my dog's spot on the floor), down a hallway, or sometimes in the middle of an apparently empty street. Is he seeing ghosts? Or not seeing at all, but sensing something I'm unaware of? Was whatever experience he was having unique to him, or would any dog have had the same reaction to my night-darkened window? I started to think about how we define 'normal' ability, and by extension, disability, which, as I state in the poem, linked to the history of my apartment building. That building was so magnetically creepy—while it had been renovated since its creation more than 100 years ago, there were odd quirks like windowpanes that made a magnificently loud sound when hit by gusts, nubs of what looked like carbon that occasionally dropped from the exposed beams in the ceiling, and once an invasion of flies seemingly from nowhere. When I started to write about these oddities that, to me, were supremely mysterious, I found myself contemplating the larger question of the 'gaseous planet of ability' that shapes all our sensory experiences. Maybe what feels like mystery is simply our bumping up against the limits of our abilities, however we might define them."

YESENIA MONTILLA is an Afro Latina poet and the daughter of immigrants. Her first collection, *The Pink Box* (Aquarius Press, 2015), was longlisted for a PEN award. Her second collection, *Muse Found in a Colonized Body*, was released in 2022 by Four Way Books. She lives in Harlem.

Of "How to Greet a Warbler," Montilla writes: "Like so many other folks I watched the video of Amy Cooper calling the police on a Black man in Central Park simply because as a bird watcher he asked that she keep her dog on a leash. It is a miracle that Christian Cooper survived that incident. It is unfathomable to think that a call to the authorities could lead to someone's death; but this is a reality for Black people in America. A few days after I came across a warbler in Riverside Park and just felt like he was speaking about the incident, too, the poem was born at that moment."

JULIA ANNA MORRISON was born in Atlanta, Georgia, in 1988 and received her MFA from the University of Iowa. She teaches screenwriting at the University of Iowa and coedits *Two Peach* with Catherine Pond.

Morrison writes: "It's strange to me that my brother, whose loss when I was young brought me to poetry in the first place, appears in what is essentially a poem about the end of a relationship. I must have gone into 'Myths About Trees' looking for a way through that pain and it led me back to that first death, to the language-world I crafted in the aftermath—all snow and trees and water. I can see how language was saving me in 'Myths About Trees' again. The poem is a shelter, as much about writing poetry as it is about the power of myth, of telling stories, inventing landscapes, of recasting and accepting a new narrative."

SARA MUMOLO was born in Anaheim, California, in 1981. She is the author of *Day Counter* (Omnidawn, 2018) and *Mortar* (Omnidawn,

2013). She is director of diversity and outreach programs for Stanford Online High School and Stanford Pre-Collegiate Studies. In 2021, she was a Poetry & the Senses Fellow at the UC Berkeley's Arts & Research Center. She received her MFA from Saint Mary's College of California.

Mumolo writes: "'Trauma Note,' published originally in *Maiden Magazine*, recalls the 2017 Northern California firestorm. I use the writing itself as a means to question how traumas emerge from, and merge with, the emergencies erupting around us—climate, cultural crises, and more. As the lines come, I type them into my iPhone Notes. A dashed-off note lassos the magnitude of trauma and feels less consequential living in an object I stick in my back pocket. That dash may help to avoid retriggering dangerous behaviors, memories, or denials. How does one touch a 'trigger' and not 'fire' it as a 'weapon'? In the series of Trauma Notes, from which this poem is taken, I document what is both known and unknowable, as I ask myself, what authenticity can be offered through a documentary mode? The poem remembers a lived experience, sometimes others' and sometimes mine, but it is not the lived experience."

LUISA MURADYAN was born in Odessa, Ukraine, in 1986. She is the author of *American Radiance* (University of Nebraska Press), which won the 2017 *Prairie Schooner* Book Prize. She holds a PhD in poetry from the University of Houston and is a member of the Cheburashka Collective.

Of "Quoting the Bible," Muradyan writes: "Like so many parents of young children, I have been holding my breath these past few years. This poem felt like an exhale, a reminder to keep moving forward into the life we have been given."

ROBIN MYERS was born in New York in 1987 and works as a translator. Her two poetry collections, not yet published in the United States, have been translated into Spanish and issued in Mexico, Argentina, Chile, and Spain. Recent poetry translations from Spanish include *Copy* by Dolores Dorantes (Wave Books, 2022), *Another Life* by Daniel Lipara (Eulalia Books, 2021), and *The Science of Departures* by Adalber Salas Hernández (Kenning Editions, 2021). She lives in Mexico

City, where she is working on a new collection of poems and a book of essays about translating poetry.

Of "Diego de Montemayor," Myers writes: "On the Mexican branch of my family tree, I have an ancestor who committed many atrocious crimes. He's probably not the only one, but he's the one I know about. I wrote this poem thinking about the ways in which power erases vast swaths of human life from generational narratives for the sake of erecting its monuments—its History—and about colonial violence and gender violence as forces that have always gone hand in hand. But I also wrote it thinking about family, in a more intimate sense, as a mystery through and through: immeasurable, unsettling, marked both by what we're told about where we come from and by everything we'll never know."

SHARON OLDS was born in San Francisco in 1942. Her latest collection, *Balladz*, was published by Alfred A. Knopf in 2022.

Of "Best Friend Ballad," Olds writes: "An invitation to visit Emily Dickinson's home, and do some writing in her room, inspired the quatrain to reappear at the surface of some of my poems from where it had been, from the beginning, as my deep grid, submerged. This, and the initial eighteen months of the COVID-19 quarantine, led to *Balladz*."

CYNTHIA PARKER-OHENE is a poet, abolitionist, cultural worker, and therapist. She received her MFA in creative writing at Saint Mary's College of California, where she was awarded a Chester Aaron Scholarship for Excellence in Creative Writing. She has won the San Francisco Foundation/Nomadic Press Poetry Prize and received fellowships and support from Tin House, Callaloo, and Juniper. Her work appears in the anthologies *Black Nature: Four Centuries of African American Nature Poetry*, and *The Ringing Ear: Black Poets Lean South*. Her book *Daughters of Harriet* was published in 2022 by the Center for Literary Publishing, University Press of Colorado. *Drapetomania* won the Backbone Press Chapbook Competition in 2017.

Of "In Virginia," Parker-Ohene writes: "Pearlie represents the cadre of Black women who toiled in the kitchens of white women. Black women were unable to spend time with family, because they labored to pay for the room in which the white woman would be free to perform, in a room to be authentic and to be who she was meant to be. I thought of the women in my family, 'The Kelley' women whose bodies were committed to racism and capitalism. In my work, I am most concerned with the Pearlies who were required to center the needs of white women and their families at their expense. It is an amalgamation of what Black women were willing to sacrifice in order to nurture their families and ensure the survival of the Black community. This poem is a love story; Pearlie is who I see when we speak about the layers of Black love."

CECILY PARKS was born in New York in 1976. She is the author of two poetry collections and editor of the anthology *The Echoing Green: Poems of Fields, Meadows, and Grasses* (Everyman's Library, 2016).

Of "Pandemic Parable," Parks writes: "My husband, a family physician, never stopped going to work when the COVID-19 pandemic arrived in the spring of 2020. I spent long days at home with our twin seven-year-old daughters. This poem captures some of the activity and anxiety of those days, but it also draws on the long solitary walks that I was able to take on weekends or on weekday evenings when my husband came home. On those walks, I learned the names of all the poisonous flowers in my neighborhood, and I often visited a fence covered in jasmine. In hindsight, I was also composing this poem, a third-person thought experiment of another mother who walks away from her home and the people in it as if to run away for good. I think of the poem as a parable because the mother and her daughters are each, in their own way, learning lessons about vanishment."

D. A. POWELL was born in Albany, Georgia, in 1963. His most recent collection of poems is *Atlas T* (Rescue Press, 2020). He received the National Book Critics Circle Award in poetry in 2013 and the 2019 John Updike Award from the American Academy of Arts and Letters. He teaches at University of San Francisco and watches way too many movies.

Of "Elegy on Fire," Powell writes: "It was the third or fourth month of Fourth of July in 2020 when I was finally fed up with the fireworks. An alarm was going off somewhere and I couldn't tell if it was a car alarm triggered by one of the endless explosions folks were amusing themselves with or if it was my own fire alarm inside my building. I am rarely one who feels 'I gotta write this' but I felt I had to write this. This feeling of anxiety that echoed back through many fire alarms and many explosions that shaped my fear of flames. It came out of me like a demon sent packing. Sometimes poetry is a way to gather up all the negative energy that is bedeviling you and cast it out. This was that kind of exorcism.

"And then all I had to do was edit it for clarity and length, as you do sometimes with prose."

VALENCIA ROBIN was born in Atlanta, Georgia, in 1968. Her debut collection of poems, *Ridiculous Light*, won Persea Books' Lexi Rudnitsky First Book Prize (2018) and was named one of *Library Journal*'s best poetry books of 2019. A Cave Canem Fellow, she has won a 2021 National Endowment for the Arts Fellowship and the Emily Clark Balch Prize in Poetry. A painter as well as a poet, she holds an MFA in creative writing from the University of Virginia and an MFA in art and design from the University of Michigan, where she cofounded GalleryDAAS, a gallery and arts program devoted to artists of the African diaspora. Robin lives in Charlottesville, Virginia, where she is a co-director of the UVA Young Writers Workshop.

Robin writes: "'After Graduate School' was written in between finishing my MFA at the University of Virginia and starting my current position as a co-director of the UVA Young Writers Workshop. And ask me what I would've done to attend a summer writing camp like the one I now run, to have discovered my love for poetry as a teenager rather than in midlife. That's part of the backstory that's hinted at in the poem—I'm a late bloomer. And while facing all the unknowns after finishing school can be scary regardless of age, being so much older than the average grad student brought its own anxieties. That is, while my classmates were lamenting the idea of moving back in with their parents, for me and no doubt anyone from the working class who'd managed to claw their way into a professional job like the one I left to study poetry, the stakes felt much higher. None of which is in the poem. What's in the poem is the thing that saved me that year. Walking. The simple power of putting one foot in front of the other while observing anything and everything along the way. Hippocrates said, *If you are in a bad mood, go for a walk. If you are still in a bad mood, go for another walk.* Exactly."

MICHAEL ROBINS was born in Portland, Oregon, in 1976. His most recent books are *People You May Know* (Saturnalia Books, 2020) and *The Bright Invisible* (Saturnalia, 2022). He lives in the Portage Park neighborhood of Chicago.

Of "The Remaining Facts," Robins writes: "On the first day of summer, two years ago, I wrote a prose poem. The next day I wrote another, and on the next day yet another. So began a record of what would become a season marked by loss and grief: we said goodbye to our dog, I visited my father for the final time, and then my partner died after she flew home early from our vacation on the Outer Banks. She was forty-one years old. I would of course give this poem back, along with all the poems ever written, if our children could have another hour with their mother."

MATTHEW ROHRER is the author of ten books of poems, most recently *The Others*, which won the Believer Book Award, and *The Sky Contains the Plans*, both published by Wave Books. He was a cofounder of *Fence* magazine and Fence Books, and teaches at NYU. He is a proud citizen of Brooklyn.

Of "Follow Them," Rohrer writes: "*It is the honorable characteristic of poetry that its materials are to be found in every subject which can interest the human mind*—(Wordsworth). And that includes sports. A sustained interest in sports is no different from a sustained interest in opera or chamber music. The famous Olmec heads are wearing the leather helmets of ball players. The Mayan epic the *Popol Vuh* is about a ball game. This poem was written before the Michigan Wolverines finally beat the hated Ohio State Buckeyes after a drought of ten years."

PATRICK ROSAL, born in 1969 in Belleville, New Jersey, is an interdisciplinary artist, composer, and author of five full-length poetry collections including *The Last Thing: New and Selected Poems* (Persea Books), which was named one of the best books of 2021 by *The Boston Globe*. He has received fellowships from the John Simon Guggenheim Foundation, the National Endowment for the Arts, Fulbright Research

Scholar Program, and the Civitella Ranieri Residency. He is the inaugural Campus Co-Director of the Mellon-funded Institute for the Study of Global Racial Justice at Rutgers-Camden, New Jersey, where he is a professor of English and coordinates the Quilting Water Initiative. A winner of the Lenore Marshall Prize from the Academy of American Poets, he has performed as poet and musician in Europe, Africa, Asia, and throughout the Americas at venues that include Lincoln Center, NJPAC, and the Cabrillo housing projects for agricultural workers. His writing and performance career spans more than twenty years.

Of "La Época En Que Hay Olvida," Rosal writes: "The title of this poem is taken from Pablo Neruda's 'No Hay Olvido (Sonata),' which contains lines that have been a touchstone for all of my writing, collaborations, and compositions: '*Si me preguntáis de dónde vengo, tengo que conversar con cosas rotas.*' (If you ask me where I'm from, I must speak with broken things). It's a reminder that nothing is whole; everything is incomplete, despite the rampant mythologies of wholeness and perfection. The world is a continuity of fragments, which is to say—lyrical—as is memory itself. It is forgetting that marks the beginning and end of memory (or is woven throughout it). Similarly, silence marks the beginning and end of our singing. So this poem, like other lyric poems, is a composition of broken memory and broken song."

ERIKA L. SÁNCHEZ is a Mexican American poet, novelist, and essayist. Her debut poetry collection, *Lessons on Expulsion*, was published by Graywolf Press in 2017, and was a finalist for the PEN America Open Book Award. Her debut young adult novel, *I Am Not Your Perfect Mexican Daughter*, published in 2017 by Knopf Books for Young Readers, was a *New York Times* bestseller and a National Book Award finalist. It is being made into a film directed by America Ferrera. A memoir, *Crying in the Bathroom*, was published by Viking in 2022. Sanchez was a 2017–2019 Princeton Arts Fellow, a 2018 recipient of the 21st Century Award from the Chicago Public Library Foundation, and a 2019 recipient of a National Endowment for the Arts Fellowship. She is currently the Sor Juana Inés de la Cruz Chair at DePaul University.

Of "Departure," Sánchez writes: "This poem was an attempt to work through trauma. Though writing has always been a way for me to make sense of my life, I believed I could never write about such a painful experience. . . . And then one day I did."

ALEXIS SEARS is the author of *Out of Order* (Autumn House Press, 2022), winner of the 2021 Donald Justice Poetry Prize. She was born in 1995 in Los Angeles, California.

Sears writes: "I'm biracial (half-black, half-white), but my father passed when I was eleven, so I grew up without much exposure to black culture. 'Hair Sestina' is about my experience teaching myself about what it means to be a mixed-race black woman."

DIANE SEUSS's most recent collection is *frank: sonnets* (Graywolf Press, 2021), which received the National Book Critics Award. *Still Life with Two Dead Peacocks and a Girl* (Graywolf, 2018) was a finalist for the National Book Critics Circle Award and the *Los Angeles Times* Book Prize in Poetry. *Four-Legged Girl* appeared from Graywolf in 2015. *Wolf Lake, White Gown Blown Open* (University of Massachusetts Press, 2010) received the Juniper Prize. She was a 2020 Guggenheim Fellow and received the John Updike Award from the American Academy of Arts and Letters in 2021. Born in Michigan City, Indiana, in 1956, she was raised by a single mother in rural Michigan, which she continues to call home.

Seuss writes: "'Modern Poetry' describes the landscape and culture of what was called modern poetry, and the modern poetry classroom, in the 1970s, when I was a scholarship student at a rigorous liberal arts college, straight out of a Midwestern, rural, working-class town and high school. The speaker, a version of me, encounters the Western Canon (with a seductive, disconcerting sneak peek at Sylvia Plath's *Ariel*), and then a course called Women's Literature (it had to be announced in those days) at the public university down the hill. I wasn't innocent but I was guileless, unschooled in the world of ideas. I wasn't ready. When are we ever ready for poetry? And what can poetry be in the face of real-life violence and heartache? This poem is a little epic of the most rattling year of my formal education."

Born in Framingham, Massachusetts, in 1972, PRAGEETA SHARMA is the author of *Grief Sequence* (Wave Books, 2019) among other works. She is the founder of Thinking Its Presence, an interdisciplinary conference on race, creative writing, and artistic and aesthetic practices. She is the Henry G. Lee '37 Professor of English at Pomona College.

Of "Widowing," Sharma writes: "There's intimacy in knowing and living with your partner's vices, but it takes its toll. I felt very isolated in my experience of knowing and loving my late husband Dale and I felt true intimacy with him by accepting many of his flaws—some were too hard and costly—for so long before he was sick. After he died, I learned about one last secret flaw, infidelity, and that's what undid me. The flaws I had learned to accept took new meanings with infidelity introduced to the mix. I had to come to terms with the fact that secrets, addiction, infidelity, and self-loathing were intertwined and made him increasingly unknowable to me. I learned of so much of this when I searched his computer and art studio, all hidden from me when he was alive. I wrote this poem to examine what risky disclosure feels like to me. Could the poem hold uncomfortable truths so I could release them? There are many resources for widows out there but many less when it's about a complicated grieving process, when *you stop feeling like you knew your spouse* and death arrives before you can talk it out or confront. So the poem became a place to process secondary grieving. I allude to this in *Grief Sequence* but after much healing and therapy, I'm addressing it more explicitly with my new manuscript-in-progress, *Onement Won*. I try to examine who I am as I write through disclosure to a kind of interior sense of closure."

CHARLES SIMIC is a poet, essayist, and translator. He is the recipient of many awards, including the Pulitzer Prize, the Griffin Prize, and a MacArthur Fellowship. In 2007 Simic was appointed the fifteenth Poet Laureate Consultant in Poetry to the Library of Congress. His most recent volume of poetry is *Come Closer and Listen* (Ecco, 2019). *The Life of Images*, a book of his selected prose, was published by Ecco in 2015. He was the guest editor of *The Best American Poetry 1992*.

JAKE SKEETS is Diné from the Navajo Nation. He was born in 1991 in a small border town called Gallup, New Mexico. He is the author of *Eyes Bottle Dark with a Mouthful of Flowers* (Milkweed Editions, 2019), winner of the National Poetry Series, Kate Tufts Discovery Award, American Book Award, and Whiting Award.

Of "Anthropocene: A Dictionary," Skeets writes: "A call to save the land is a call to save the hundreds of Indigenous languages and cultures that exist across the world. This poem started as a response to the many dictionaries that exist on Diné Bizaad, the Navajo language, and the increasing rates of wildfires on the Navajo Nation. I wanted a translation that was rooted in experience that could act as a window to what is happening around us. Poetry offers us the unique ability to witness the world in truly universal ways."

JESSICA Q. STARK was born in Simi Valley, California, in 1986. Her first full-length poetry collection, *Savage Pageant*, was published by Birds in 2020 and was named one of the best poetry books of that year by *The Boston Globe* and *Hyperallergic*. She is a poetry editor for *AGNI* and the comics editor for *Honey Literary*. She teaches at the University of North Florida.

Of "Hungry Poem with Laughter Coming from an Unknown Source," Stark writes: "Jessica Q. Stark was struck by a vehicle when she was a young girl. They said her body flew up and over her kid-sized bicycle and landed eight feet away into the mouth of a suburban driveway. They said she looked dead. This was all hearsay—from neighbors, family—because she doesn't remember a thing, honestly. She doesn't even remember when they fitted the cast on her collarbone a day later or how it felt to wear it for eight weeks. In fact, she doesn't remember a lot about the year she died. She does remember there was a large settlement for the adults involved. Do you think she's dead? She remembers that she said to a neighbor a year later: 'But what exactly does a dead girl look like?' What I mean to say is: What do you think they bought with the money?"

ALINA STEFANESCU was born in Romania and lives in Birmingham, Alabama. *Every Mask I Tried On*, her debut fiction collection, won the 2018 Brighthorse Books Prize. Recent books include a creative nonfiction chapbook, *Ribald* (Bull City Press, 2020), and *Dor* (Wandering Aengus Press, 2021). She still can't believe any of this. More online at www.alinastefanescuwriter.com.

Of "Little Time," Stefanescu writes: "Let's walk, he said—as the glossolalia of pandemic headlines overwhelmed the house. This intensified sense of time amplified the silent divisions, the unsustainable dichotomy of public/private, the instability of expertise, the anxiety of small children, the privatized pain of American life, the stacked alienations, tottering—and the virtual-schooling son, practicing a piano sonata. I kept hearing something smaller, a *sonatina*, a tinier form of the parlor song, the marriage sonata, a nakedness seeking a melodic line. A mom dies in her sleep; another one drowns; another waits for the doctors to diagnose her fate: we wait for words to build livable stories for those who love us, for those who believe they cannot live without us in the sun, in the room, in the poem. The problem with life is duration. The problem with being human is preexisting conditionals, valences of lost time, Proust in a bed, trying to finish the book. The restless writer wants to run away. The poem wants to go for a walk and say the unspeakable: tiny steps, held breaths, puddles of silence amid the swarm of screens and digital selves. The lover invites you to walk into the terror, but the *fire*—the midnight of the poem—this part we must walk alone."

GERALD STERN was born in Pittsburgh, Pennsylvania, in 1925. He is the author of nearly thirty books of essays and poetry, the most recent of which is *Blessed as We Were: Late Selected and New Poems* (W. W. Norton, 2020).

BIANCA STONE was born in Burlington, Vermont, in 1983. She is the author of *What Is Otherwise Infinite* (Tin House, 2022), *The Mobius Strip Club of Grief* (Tin House, 2018), *Someone Else's Wedding Vows* (Octopus Books and Tin House, 2014) and the children's book *A Little Called Pauline*, with text by Gertrude Stein (Penny Candy Books, 2020). She teaches poetry and is creative director at the Ruth Stone House in Vermont.

Of "The Infant's Eyes," Stone writes: "Essentially this poem is about the strangeness of being *seen*. Being seen by something that is part of you, yet totally alien: your own infant. It is an incredible moment to be looked at with such depth by such a new thing in this world, but it is also very frightening—we long to be seen for who we are, we are also ashamed of who we are. And neither of those truths are very articulated in our daily thoughts. They lie under the surface—the infant who looks deeply at the mother is something out of time, foreign, new—and yet the most natural, ancient relationship known to humans."

MICHAEL TEIG was born in Franklin, Pennsylvania, in 1968. He is the author of *There's a Box in the Garage You Can Beat with a Stick* (BOA Editions, 2013) and *Big Back Yard* (BOA, 2003), which won the inaugural A. Poulin, Jr. Poetry Prize. He lives in Easthampton, Massachusetts.

Of "At This Point My Confusion," Teig writes: "After my son's birth, we received among other things a couple of garbage bags full of hand-me-down clothes from a relatively well-off friend, including many finely made little pants. I recall feeling at the time 'These tiny fancy pants are amazing!' and, equally, 'I'm in no way ready for this.' I don't remember what I was thinking when I wrote this poem but when I read it now, I see that it contains that confusion—family history and revision, hope for my son, and, however secondhand or implausible, grace. I like the possibility, too, that those pants are still in the world, galloping off."

OCEAN VUONG is the author of *Time Is a Mother* (Penguin, 2022), the novel *On Earth We're Briefly Gorgeous* (Penguin, 2019), and the debut poetry collection *Night Sky with Exit Wounds* (Copper Canyon Press, 2016). Born in 1988 in Saigon, Vietnam, he lives in Northampton, Massachusetts.

WILLIAM WALTZ was born in Wapakoneta, Ohio. He is the author of *Adventures in the Lost Interiors of America* (Cleveland State University Poetry Center, 2013), *Confluence of Mysterious Origins* (Factory Hollow Press, 2012), and *Zoo Music* (Slope Editions, 2004). He is the founder and editor of *Conduit*. Waltz lives with his family in Saint Paul, Minnesota, near the Mississippi River and its fossil-strewn bluffs.

Of "In a dark time, the eye begins to see," Waltz writes: "The title is borrowed from a Theodore Roethke poem that I turned to during the hellacious spring of 2020. I kept saying it can't get any worse, but it did. So I quit saying that and wrote this poem, which tries to imagine rebounding after hitting bottom."

ROBERT WHITEHEAD was born in New Jersey in 1988 and received his MFA from Washington University in Saint Louis. He lives in Philadelphia and works as a graphic designer. More at robertmwhitehead.com.

Of "Hi, How Are You," Whitehead writes: "There was a time when the only reason I would have gotten out of bed was to admire the flowers that grew around my house in West Philadelphia. Then I wrote this poem. The triangle is both the strongest geometrical shape and the mathematical symbol for change."

EL WILLIAMS III was born in St. Louis, Missouri, in 1989. He has received fellowships and scholarships from Cave Canem, Community of Writers, Tin House, and the Watering Hole. He currently lives in Bloomington, where he is a dual MFA/MA candidate in poetry and African American & African diaspora studies at Indiana University.

Of "Elegy for the Gnat," Williams writes: "I drafted this poem in June of 2020, while attending a virtual writing retreat, a few months into the global COVID-19 pandemic. Isolated in my apartment with groceries and things that were said to sustain me, keep me as I stayed away from other humans, I lavished, as I do each season but especially summer, in the pleasure of fruit. As we know, with fruit come gnats and/or fruit flies. However, in the midst of so much death (COVID-19 patients, Black and Brown people being victims of police brutality, white supremacist terrorism, etc.), so many transitions, and so much loneliness, my relationship to other humans, yes, but also, to gnats and/or fruit flies, and nature, in general, began to shift. 'Why kill a thing?' I began to ask myself, 'The gnats are only visiting.' Yet, one evening as I sat to write with a gnat floating about in my writing space, I brought to the table two fingers of bourbon. By the third sip, I recognized that the gnat, too, had indulged or gotten lost or simply, through a combination of things, became loss."

PHILLIP B. WILLIAMS, a Chicago native born in 1986, is the author of *Thief in the Interior* (Alice James, 2016), winner of the 2017 Kate Tufts Discovery Award and a 2017 Lambda Literary award, and *Mutiny* (Penguin Poetry, 2021). He received a 2017 Whiting Award and fellowship from the Radcliffe Institute for Advanced Study.

Of "Final Poem for My Father Misnamed in My Mouth," Williams writes: "I wrote this poem to end all future poems about my father written purely as addict and absent. I love him very much now that I've grown to understand the situation of his life, and though much inner-child work needs to be done, I would prefer to do so outside of the page and with more care that honors the life he was able to live."

ELIZABETH WILLIS was born in Bahrain in 1961. Her most recent book, *Alive*, was published by New York Review Books in 2015. Other books include *Address* (Wesleyan University Press, 2011), recipient of the PEN New England/L. L. Winship Prize for Poetry; *Meteoric Flowers* (Wesleyan, 2007); *Turneresque* (Burning Deck, 2003); and *The Human Abstract* (Penguin, 1995). She teaches at the Iowa Writers' Workshop.

Of "What Else in Art Do You Pay For," Willis writes: "One July I was teaching in the Naropa summer program for a week organized around the topic 'Fire and Brimstone.' It was a hot summer, the world was on fire, and the rhetoric of ecological and spiritual end-times was everywhere. That week CAConrad and I sat together in a conversation that has continued in various forms, about the kinds of work that poets are—for reasons that are not always obvious—called to do.

"I think of poems as stepping into an ongoing call-and-response with the world. I'm interested in what happens when we catch a signal we don't understand, whether it's filtered through the heaps of sense data we inherit or sought out from resources beyond ordinary perception. I want to reckon with the timeline of art, on one hand, and of the garbage I leave behind, on the other: what I use and what uses me. I'm interested in an art that doesn't turn away.

"Over the past few years, I've often returned to Frank O'Hara's line that 'In times of crisis we must all decide again and again whom we love.' Love's risks open us to heartbreak and to the knowledge of our failures as individuals, as a culture, as a species. That's what makes its brilliance so indelible. I suppose that's why Hank Williams shows up in the middle of all this with his high-lonesome cry. Pain transformed into art is still pain.

"More on the above can be found in my essay 'Notes From and On a Landscape,' available for free at thevolta.org."

MARK WUNDERLICH is the author of four books of poems, the most recent of which is *God of Nothingness* (Graywolf Press, 2021). A 2021 Guggenheim Foundation Fellow, he is the director of the Bennington Writing Seminars in Vermont, and lives in New York's Hudson Valley.

Of "First, Chill," Wunderlich writes: "This poem was written during a year when eight people I was close to—friends, mentors, relatives, and finally my father—all died. I spent much of the year comprehending those losses, and I found that many of my usual pleasures were compromised or altered by the grief I was feeling. Poetry can't fix much, but it's really good at organizing language around the great fact and mystery of death, and if you're a poet, you also get to write your way toward some state in which experience has meaning; poems are the monuments we make to that practice."

DEAN YOUNG was born in Columbia, Pennsylvania, in 1955. His most recent book of poems is *Solar Perplexus* (Copper Canyon Press, 2019). He writes: "The older I get, the shorter my bio gets."

Of "Spark Theory," he writes: "Every spark has its own idea but they all still end up swallowed by darkness."

FELICIA ZAMORA is the author of six books of poetry, including *I Always Carry My Bones*, winner of the 2020 Iowa Poetry Prize (University of Iowa Press, 2021); *Quotient* (Tinderbox Editions, 2022); *Body of Render*, Benjamin Saltman Award winner (Red Hen Press, 2020); and *Of Form & Gather*, Andrés Montoya Poetry Prize winner (University of Notre Dame Press, 2017). A CantoMundo and Ragdale Foundation Fellow, she won the 2020 C.P. Cavafy Prize from *Poetry International*, the Wabash Prize for Poetry, and the Tomaž Šalamun Prize. She is an assistant professor of poetry at the University of Cincinnati and associate poetry editor for the *Colorado Review*. She was born in Iowa Falls, Iowa, in 1978.

Of "Chris Martin Sings 'Shiver' & I Shiver: A Poem for Madam Vice President," Zamora writes: "When I was little, no one said, 'You can be anything you want to be, Felicia.' No one told me, 'Dream,' let alone follow my dreams. Growing up in poverty as a Mexican girl in all-white spaces, I felt the projections of reductive and harmful narratives hurled at me—about who society thought I should be. I was less than an expectation to them. But I resisted with my imagination. I dreamed nonetheless. When this country elected Madam Vice President Kamala Harris, I cried in front of the tv. I know I wasn't alone in this reaction. I cried because a woman of color being vice president meant my dreams manifest to the real. I cried because the impossible became possible. I cried for the difficulties Vice President Harris would certainly face. I cried for a lifetime of waiting for the impossible to become possible—the ridiculous slowness in which liberation for BIWOC is occurring. I cried for my own hard memories and for the hope that future brown and Black girls will feel a world that supports and loves them. I cried for the futurity of possibility. Over a week later, while on 275 to Dayton, I listened to Coldplay and the idea of 'shiver' took on a whole new meaning for me. I began to shiver, in mind and organs. I shivered with a type of overwhelming clarity—*keep fighting*. What began to unfold was a love poem to all women. A love poem sparked not by one event, but by the compounding work of women throughout history to pave a path for us as humans. I hope readers find the love in this poem as much as the ache."

JENNY ZHANG was born in Shanghai and grew up in New York. She is the author of the poetry collections *Dear Jenny, We Are All Find* (Octopus Books, 2012) and *My Baby First Birthday* (Tin House Books, 2020), and the story collection *Sour Heart* (Lenny, 2017).

Of "under the chiming bell," Zhang writes: "My first artist residency was in the woods. So much beauty on stolen land. I looked at photos of former residents over the decades. Does it need to be said what they looked like and who gets to breathe fresh air? I was used to being the one cooking and serving and cleaning after others and now, I was on the other side. Being 'chosen' for these kinds of experiences is confusing. To go from scarcity and deprivation to being waited on warps the psyche and bears no relation to actually redistributing resources or changing the material conditions for the collective."

MAGAZINES WHERE THE POEMS WERE FIRST PUBLISHED

The Academy of American Poets Poem-a-Day, 2021 guest eds. Kazim Ali, Fatimah Asghar, Jane Hirshfield, Linda Hogan, Ilya Kaminsky, and Safia Sinclair. www.poets.org

The Adirondack Review, poetry ed. Nicholas Samaras. www.theadirondack review.com

The Adroit Journal, poetry eds. Emily Cinquemani, Chris Crowder, Kate Gaskin, Lisa Hiton, Eugenia Leigh, and Francisco Márquez. www. theadroitjournal.org

Air/Light, ed. David L. Ulin. www.airlightmagazine.org

Alaska Quarterly Review, editor-in-chief Ronald Spatz. www.aqreview.org

Alta, editor and publisher William R. Hearst III. www.altaonline.com

The American Poetry Review, ed. Elizabeth Scanlon. www.aprweb.org

The Atlantic, poetry ed. David Barber. www.theatlantic.com

The Believer, poetry ed. Jericho Brown. www.believermag.com

Bennington Review, ed. Michael Dumanis. www.benningtonreview.org

Blackbird, eds. Mary Flinn and M. A. Keller. www.blackbird.vcu.edu

Colorado Review, poetry eds. Donald Revell, Sasha Steensen, Camille T. Dungy, and Matthew Cooperman. www.coloradoreview.colostate.edu

Conduit, editor-in-chief William D. Waltz. www.conduit.org

Copper Nickel, poetry eds. Brian Barker and Nicky Beer. www.copper -nickel.org

The Cortland Review, poetry eds. Anna Catone, Gustavo Hernandez, and Annie Schumacher. www.cortlandreview.com

Court Green, eds. Aaron Smith and Tony Trigilio. www.courtgreen.net

The Georgia Review, poetry cd. Soham Patel. www.thegeorgiareview.com

Guernica, poetry ed. Erica Wright. www.guernicamag.com

Harper's, poetry ed. Ben Lerner. www.harpers.org

Hobart After Dark, poetry eds. Doug Paul Case, Dorothy Chan, and Emma Heldman. www.havehashad.com

Incessant Pipe, ed. Clay Ventre. www.incessantpipe.wordpress.com

Iterant, editor-in-chief Walter J. Stone. www.iterant.org

jubilat, eds. Caryl Pagel and Emily Pettit. www.jubilat.org

The Kenyon Review, ed. Nicole Terez Dutton. www.kenyonreview.org

Literary Matters, poetry ed. Armen Davoudian. www.literarymatters.org

Maiden Magazine, eds. Caroline O'Connor Thomas and Brittany Wason. www.maiden-magazine.com

The Massachusetts Review, poetry eds. Franny Choi and Nathan McClain. www.massreview.org

Mississippi Review, editor-in-chief Adam Clay. www.sites.usm.edu /mississippi-review

The Missouri Review, poetry ed. Jacob Hall. www.missourireview.com

The New Republic, poetry ed. Rowan Ricardo Phillips. www.newrepublic .com

The New York Review of Books, executive ed. Jana Prikryl. www .nybooks.com

The New York Times Magazine, 2020–2021 poetry ed. Reginald Dwayne Betts. www.nytimes.com/column/magazine-poem

The New Yorker, poetry ed. Kevin Young. www.newyorker.com

Northwest Review, poetry eds. Michael McGriff and Natalie Staples. www.nwreview.org

The Paris Review, poetry ed. Vijay Seshadri. www.theparisreview.org

Pleiades, poetry eds. Jenny Molberg, Erin Adair-Hodges, and Caitlin Cowan. www.pleiadesmag.com

Ploughshares, poetry ed. John Skoyles. www.pshares.org

Poetry, interim coeditors Fred Sasaki and Lindsay Garbutt.www.poetry foundation.org/poetrymagazine

Poetry Daily, www.poems.com

The Rumpus, poetry eds. Cortney Lamar Charleston and Carolina Ebeid. www.therumpus.net

Salmagundi, eds. Robert Boyers and Peg Boyers. www.salmagundi .skidmore.edu

The Tiny, eds. Gina Myers and Emma Brown Sanders. www.thetiny mag.com

The Threepenny Review, ed. Wendy Lesser. www.threepennyreview.com

TriQuarterly, poetry ed. Daniel Fliegel. www.triquarterly.org

Virginia Quarterly Review, poetry ed. Gregory Pardlo. www.vqronline.org

West Branch, poetry ed. Sylvia Jones. www.westbranch.blogs.bucknell.edu

West Trestle Review, poetry eds. Joan Kwon Glass and Annie Stenzel. www.westtrestlereview.com

The Yale Review, ed. Meghan O'Rourke. www.yalereview.yale.edu

Zyzzyva, ed. Laura Cogan. www.zyzzyva.org

ACKNOWLEDGMENTS

The series editor thanks Mark Bibbins for his invaluable assistance. Warm thanks go also to Denise Duhamel, Amy Gerstler, Dana Gioia, Stacey Harwood, Major Jackson, Mary Jo Salter, and Terence Winch; to Glen Hartley and Lynn Chu of Writers' Representatives; and to Kathy Belden, David Stanford Burr, Daniel Cuddy, Kathryn Kenney-Peterson, and Mia O'Neill at Scribner.

Grateful acknowledgment is made of the magazines in which these poems first appeared and the magazine editors who selected them. A sincere attempt has been made to locate all copyright holders. Unless otherwise noted, copyright to the poems is held by the individual poets.

Aria Aber, "America" from *Poetry*. Reprinted by permission of the poet.

Raymond Antrobus, "Text and Image" from *All the Names Given*. © 2021 by Raymond Antrobus. Reprinted by permission of Tin House Books. Also appeared in *The Rumpus*.

Dara Barrois/Dixon, "Remembering" from *Incessant Pipe*. Reprinted by permission of the poet.

E. C. Belli, "Vows" from *A Sleep That Is Not Our Sleep*. © 2022 by E. C. Belli. Reprinted by permission of Anhinga Press. Also appeared in Poem-a-Day.

Oliver Baez Bendorf, "What the Dead Can Do" from *West Branch*. Reprinted by permission of the poet.

Kristin Bock, "Gaslighter" from *Glass Bikini*. © 2021 by Kristin Bock. Reprinted by permission of The Permissions Company, Inc., on behalf of Tupelo Press. Also appeared in *Iterant*.

William Brewer, "Anthony Bourdain" from *Zyzzyva*. Reprinted by permission of the poet.

Jericho Brown, "Inaugural" from *The New York Times Magazine*. Reprinted by permission of the poet.

James Cagney, "Proof" from *Alta*. Reprinted by permission of the poet.